M000238927

WHERE SOCIAL WORK CAN LEAD YOU

JOURNEYS INTO, AROUND AND EVEN OUT OF SOCIAL WORK

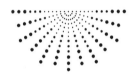

AMANDA FORDHAM   ASHLEY ABRAMSON

BETH TYSON   CHERISH FIELDS

CHRISTINA BRODERICK   COURTNEY AABERG

DANIEL MARTIN   DEB FRANK   ELIZABETH WENDEL

GILBERT DOMALLY   HILARY N. WEAVER

JEREMY CARNEY   JESS HOEPER   JESSICA HOPE

JIHAN ALI   MICHAEL MCKNIGHT   MICHELE SNEED

NAZIA BASHA   NICOLE YOUNG   SUJEETA E. MENON

TEYA F. DAHLE   THU-HA PARK   WARREN L. GRAVER

YACENIA MURLEE Q. CRISOSTOMO

EXALTED PUBLISHING HOUSE

Copyright © 2022 by Jessica Hoeper

All rights reserved. Apart from any fair dealing for the purposes of research or private study, or criticism or rev iew as permitted under the Copyright, Designs, and Patents Act 1988, this publication may only be reproduced, stored, or transmitted, in any form or means, with the prior permission in writing of the copyright owner, or in the case of the reprographic reproduction in accordance with the terms of licenses issued by Copyright Licensing Agency. Enquires concerning reproduction outside those terms should be sent to the publisher.

Disclaimer

The publisher takes no legal responsibility for the details inside the stories of this book. The words and opinions are the writer's own, the memories they describe are their lived experience and I do not have any evidence that those stories are untrue. I've chosen to trust the authors and have not done them the disservice of fact-checking every version of events. Memoirs are stories from one person's vantage point and these experiences are unfortunately, universal and this is why we've chosen to share them in this collection.

Although the publisher and the authors have made every effort to ensure that the information in this book was correct at press time and while this publication is designed to provide accurate information in regard to the subject matter covered, the publisher and the authors assume no responsibility for errors, inaccuracies, omissions, or any other consistencies herein and hereby disclaim any liability to any party for any loss, damage, or disruption caused by errors or omissions, whether such errors or omissions results from negligence, accident, or any other cause.

CONTENTS

INTRODUCTION

Where Social Work Can Lead You, is an invitation from professionals and leaders to share in their journeys, through personal stories. Within a short number of pages, authors share some pivotal moments that shaped their journey into, around and even out of social work.

Each story is told from the author's perspective and some journeys shared contain sensitive content. Courage was required.

In this book you will find stories of journeys from long ago and journeys just beginning. Common themes within each journey include; the deep desire to be connected to others, the desire to help, the desire to see those that feel unseen, and a rise to the call for social justice.

Story telling is social action. Sharing journey stories builds the momentum to connect, to seek others' journey stories, and to see the journey stories within ourselves. This is collective building through journey stories shared.

This book serves as a professional call to action. All those who come into, around, or out of social work have a personal journey, and directly parallel, all those served by the field of social work have a journey story. Let's be reminded that the helping profession of social work was in fact built on passions professionalized.

In the National Association of Social Workers preamble, it says, "Social workers seek to enhance the capacity of people to address their own needs." The authors are participating in redefining the social work status quo, by inviting you the reader to see the person within the profession from a new vantage point.

The book begins with journey stories **_into_** social work. The journeys are all unique, with many common themes. These are just a small sample of the journey stories within the profession of social work. This is not meant as a representation of the social work collective, except in the most basic state, that all those in social work have a journey story that led them into social work.

In the middle of the book, you will find journeys shared by those **_around_** social work. You will hear from a few professionals within fields around social work such as education, psychology, and business consulting services. Social work is a collaborative profession, relying heavily on its closest partners to influence and collaboratively move the serving professions forward in thoughts, words, and deeds.

The book ends with a glimpse into a few journeys **_out of social work_**. Social work is a system. Systems are built with boundaries. Some journey stories do not fit within conformed boundaries, and to ever push boundaries to widen, you need to have boundary pushers. The journeys out of social work will invite you to consider such things as, social work's influence on the innovation of new integrative therapeutic strategies or that social work could even be an interior design strategy! System boundaries are no match for a heart on a mission!

Enjoy each of these unique journey stories. These journeys are shared as an invitation to hear how some have come into, around and even out of social work. These stories are not to be read as comparisons to your awesome unique journey story but instead to encourage you to tell yourself your own story, to seek another's journey story, and move us towards story sharing as social action!

Stories shared can change the world!

Into Social Work

1

NAZIA BASHA, MSW, CLC

LEADING TO HOME

"THIS PLACE IS much nicer than I expected!" My client expressed his joy to me as we walked out of his apartment after completing an assessment. "After months of not having a place to yourself, this is such a big change, Ms. Basha," he added. I could see the smile in his eyes behind the N95 mask as he expressed his gratitude for finding him a suitable apartment. I acknowledged his feelings: "I know the past months have been very challenging at the homeless shelter, but I'm very happy to hear that you found your home." My client exclaimed, "Yes! Thank you for your assistance and support throughout the process!" I affirmed, "You're welcome!" "We worked through the process together sir. Please keep me informed if you have any questions until our next session."

As I concluded the meeting, I smiled at the veteran and walked towards my car. Driving back to my office, I felt joy and relief in finding him a safe and secure apartment. Housing a veteran wasn't a seamless or an easy task. As a housing social worker, I experience barriers such as dealing with the veterans' unexpected medical and mental health needs, generating, and tracking numerous community referrals, meeting deadlines, and retrieving vital documents from archives while navigating service amid the COVID-19 pandemic. Sometimes I feel overwhelmed but serving the veterans who served to protect our country or 'home', makes my work meaningful.

While ruminating on my thoughts from the visit, I noticed it was lunchtime. I walked into my office and grabbed my lunch while simultaneously scrolling through my emails on my mobile phone. I opened a message from the National Association of Social Workers (NASW) and read a post: "Looking for authors to share their journey into, around, and out of social work in a book project." My curiosity led me to explore the post further because it was a writing opportunity. I enjoy writing for my personal pleasure from drama skits, essays, poetry, and short stories. As I pondered on my decision to partake in the book project, I thought about the numerous events in my life that lead me to social work. I wanted to share about my cross cultural identity, my upbringing, and the challenges I overcame to become a social worker. After further reflection, I contacted the project coordinator and publisher and discovered that I would be collaborating with other authors who will be sharing their rich stories on what led them into, out, and around social work by providing diverse perspectives to prospective students, other social workers, or individuals who are curious about the profession.

Being raised in a culture that venerates doctors, engineers, and lawyers, I hardly knew about the social work profession. Through a series of circumstances and research, I discovered social work. My path into social work allowed me to find my voice in re-writing my narrative to "lead me home." My "home" embodies my journey, and as I share my journey in this chapter, I invite you to connect with your meaning of home while learning about the dynamic profession of social work.

Home of Origin

As a child, I defined "home" by the beliefs, culture, traditions, and values of my parents. My parents were born and raised in India. However, my mother immigrated to the United States a few years before my father. After their marriage in 1983, my father joined her in pursuing the "American Dream." Within their first year of marriage, I was born in Chicago, Illinois. Then, six years later, my sister was born in Brooklyn, New York, and eleven years later, my brother was born in St. Petersburg, Florida.

Being a second-generation American, I embrace my cross-cultural identity. I admire India's rich and diverse culture that is represented in

2

the forms of architecture, art, cuisine, dance, history, language, music, movies, poetry, and religions. During my childhood, I visited India a few times and adapted well to Indian cultural norms. At the same time, I appreciated my American values of individualism, change, and egalitarianism. In my first formal writing piece, I expressed my patriotic sentiments in an essay that I wrote in seventh grade for a contest sponsored by a local notary club in New Port Richey, Florida. The essay topic was "What's Good About America" and I highlighted America's strengths as a country of freedom, liberty, and opportunity. To my surprise, I did not realize that I had won first place until the day I presented my essay in front of the committee.

However, being the first-born child, my parents had more cultural expectations of me. Their cultural expectations to maintain the ethnic and religious identity of a Muslim Indian woman were very important to them, but I struggled to meet their expectations. Moreover, my parents labeled me as being 'Americanized.' My parents defined Americanized as being independent, outgoing, and outspoken. I was reprimanded if I behaved "too Americanized," because my parents experienced microaggressions from non-immigrant Americans such as being told to "go back to their country," mocked for not having an American accent, and receiving minimal opportunities for advancement. However, despite the microaggressions, my parents continued to persevere with their goals with tenacity. But, their coping strategies and 'survival' mindset were not conducive to my personal development. During the formative years of my childhood, I witnessed turbulence within my parents' marriage that was caused by their incompatibilities, financial hardships, lack of adequate social support and resources, and trauma.

My mother's suffering from her childhood trauma and my father's struggles to cope with her distress or seek help had an impact on the family dynamics. Abuse, the dismissal of feelings and needs, lack of empathy, and not having individual boundaries were our family's norms. Plus, I believed that my parents' suffering was far greater than mine, and I adopted a narrative that dismissed my needs. Moreover, the discussion of emotional well-being, mental health or therapy is stigmatized in Indian culture because family problems are not discussed with anyone outside of the family unit. Revealing the family's difficulties and hardships means you were low in social rank in the community, and generational trauma is perpetuated by the inability to seek mental health counseling. Most members in my extended family continued to adhere to the traditional mindset, but I desired change.

I started recognizing that I had a high regard for pursuing higher education, but my mother insisted upon getting me married after I graduated from high school. Although some women in my family acquired higher education, it was not an option for me unless I was married and received my husband's consent. My husband would be arranged by my parents. Arranged marriages are commonly practiced in India and strictly followed in the conservative Muslim culture. My parents were married through the arrange-marriage system when technology was limited, so they did not communicate prior to marriage. Their marriage was a sudden and unplanned decision made by the elders who were more concerned about my parent's biological clocks than compatibility.

Despite my hesitation and after witnessing the stress in my parents' marriage, I agreed to get married through the arranged marriage framework in 2006. I was hoping I could oblige with my parents' expectations to gain their approval and love. However, I felt inauthentic because I experienced profound incompatibilities with my now ex-husband. I experienced the continuity of passive control from my mother that manipulated my choices and views. Within a few years of marriage, I filed for divorce. My divorce was not a cumbersome process, but I lacked support from my family. I was marginalized within my family and community. I recalled receiving messages that left me numb and rejected like:

"It's best if you don't show up this weekend because my uncle is visiting. I feel embarrassed having to explain about your divorce and reasons for staying unmarried. You have failed us! If you want an education without marriage, you need to move out of our house!"

With a heavy heart, I left my home of origin to build a home that honored and welcomed my existence. I did not disown my ethnic roots, but I left behind the antiquated beliefs and perspectives that no longer served me. But I needed time to release old habits or patterns that created obstacles which eventually forced me to re-write my narrative.

Re-Writing My Narrative

After leaving home, I remained in contact with my siblings who supported my decisions. I began therapy to shed awareness on my behaviors, patterns, and trauma that influenced my choices, but was operating within a survival mindset. I operated from scarcity instead of abundance by remaining in patterns of attracting and continuing relationships that avoided authentic emotional connection. I under-earned by working at low-paying and unfulfilling jobs, and adhered to spiritual or religious practices that preached rigid principles and chastised humanity.

On the other hand, I managed to graduate with a Bachelor's degree in Health Science in 2008, but struggled to find a suitable job. I worked in the retail industry selling jewelry for seven years to pay bills. Then, in January of 2014, one of my dearest friends shared a job vacancy that involved working with at-risk youth. I was intrigued by the job summary and applied. A week later, I was interviewed and hired immediately as a social service coordinator for a nonprofit agency to help at-risk youth to receive assistance for education, vocation, and transportation needs.

Between the years of 2014-2021 at the agency, I gained a wealth of knowledge and skills. I learned about case management, coaching, and devising individualized service plans to address the youth's needs and goals. My learning was accelerated by high employee turnover. There were many months where I handled eight counties in the Northeast Florida region while managing forty to eighty cases in the community and residential facilities. Many employees were quickly resigning due to the nature of working with at-risk youth from client compliance to continuous changes in agency practices to minimal resources.

Due to the high turnover, I managed large caseloads and traveled 500 miles per week while ensuring to meet the agency's standards. As a result, I experienced burnout and stress. The stress triggered frequent episodes of tachycardia or rapid heart rate that led me to the emergency room. After several tests, my results returned as normal. However, I received a $3000 bill over and above health insurance coverage. My anxiety from the billing statement was a calling to build my awareness of self-care.

The lack of self-care created a disconnect from my needs. Despite my passion in helping others, I became disconnected with my needs for health, creativity, and community. I decided to re-examine my lifestyle choices and values while learning to set boundaries. Setting boundaries came with the courage to say no even when I felt uncomfortable. I also developed a deeper appreciation for classical Indian dance that helped me tune into my mind-body connection. With the unwavering support from my dance instructor, I learned to unify the intricate dance step with the music and poetry during my dance performances.

Moreover, I began connecting with diverse groups of individuals to expand my social circle. I met artists, authors, coaches, dancers, leaders, musicians, and singers, and some even became my mentors. One of my dearest mentors is a painter who expresses healing through her artwork. With her, I'm able to share my struggles without feeling criticized or judged. Until today, she offers empathy, guidance, and her wisdom.

The more connections I made with people, I became inspired and fascinated by their personal life experiences. Hearing about their unique journeys prompted me to create a platform where people could share their stories of challenges, resilience, and strengths in hopes to inspire others in a visual series called "Challenge Me 4 U." There I challenge myself to have the courage to share my story of resilience to inspire you to honor your own narrative. Embarking on my new vision, I began interviewing individuals, local businesses, and organizations.

As I conducted interviews, I gained clarity on my values. I began valuing advocacy, human dignity, diversity, and social justice and discovered that my values aligned with the principles of social work. With my realization, I discovered that social work will give me the 'voice' to drive my vision in leading me home.

My Voice

As a coordinator, I experienced limitations in receiving the answers I was searching for, and it became clear that my curiosity aligned more with a graduate level of social work. I yearned for more knowledge and skills to comprehend the impact of socio-environmental factors on a person's life. After reading about the University of Central Florida's mission statement, flexibility to take courses online, and their official logo of 'Pegasus' that depicts a flying horse in Greek mythology embodying freedom, power, and eternal spring of imagination and creativity, I joyfully applied. One month later, I received a letter from the university welcoming me into the social work graduate program in August of 2018.

After ten years since college, I was nervous because I wanted to earn 'perfect' grades. However, as I connected more with the learning instead of the grades, my anxiety subsided. I enjoyed learning about various social work theories and intervention models. Moreover, my internships honed my knowledge of social work into practice, but burnout again visited me.

Balancing a fulltime job with the consistent employee turnover, internships, and academic work was overwhelming. Moreover, I lacked adequate time to maintain my video platform. To maintain my channel of creativity, I searched for alternative ways to present my content. I decided to shift my content to a podcast to address how burnout in the social service industry has an impact on quality of care.

On January 15, 2020, I launched my podcast. The COVID-19 pandemic that swept the globe a short time afterwards only heightened the awareness of self-care because many health care and front-line workers were facing burnout. I presented the topic from the lens of mental health and social justice and invited guest speakers to share their stories about their experiences with the pandemic.

As I experienced and witnessed the disparities in the world from the impact of the COVID-19 virus, my definition of home started to evolve. As more events unfolded during 2020, I sensed more division among people because of their differences in health, politics, and faith. The divisions made me reevaluate my social circle, and I disconnected with some people while rekindling my relationship with others. Moreover, I continued to develop friendships with fellow graduate students in which I received mutual aid and support. In one of my courses, I participated in a group activity that utilized narrative therapy by writing our story to foster healing and recovery.

I also took the time for a nonviolent communications course. Nonviolent Communication or (NVC) was a language discovered by Dr.

Marshall Rosenberg who claimed that in order to understand another human being, we must first understand our own humanity using empathy. Through empathy we understand our own behaviors, feelings, and needs.

The NVC model helped me transform my definition of home by identifying the core components that encompass my whole human experience. I found my meaning of home by focusing on my emotional and physical well-being, life experiences, social support, service, and spirituality. With this new realization, I experienced love and peace by accepting my journey as it was while continuing to heal and forgive. I felt love and gratitude for all the wonderful people who supported me on my journey including my colleagues, mentors, internship supervisors, friends, and siblings who have led me 'home.'

With love, I received my Master's in Social Work in August of 2021. After the following week of my graduation, my clinical internship supervisors appointed me to the position of housing social worker at the Veterans' Affairs HONOR Center in Gainesville, Florida. I'm honored to serve veterans in finding the home they deserve. I also earned a life coach certification from the International Coaching Federation to assist kindred individuals discover their meaning of home through their unique life purpose.

As more opportunities unfold along my social work journey, I offer my words of encouragement in hopes of co-creating the meaning of home as a society. As an American citizen, I encourage non-immigrant Americans to honor, respect, and provide equity for immigrants and naturalized Americans who co-create in building our economy's wealth. My hope is for us to appreciate cultural diversity rather than promoting assimilation.

As a daughter to immigrant parents, I encourage immigrants or first-generation Americans to honor their future generations by learning to evolve in a multicultural society while engaging in open and loving conversations using empathy.

As a second-generation Indian American, I encourage future generation Indian Americans to honor your ethnicity as a strength within your cross-cultural identity.

Pearl of Wisdom

"We can truly connect with others by understanding our humanity, then I believe we can facilitate systemic change collaboratively to help lead each other home."

~ Nazia Basha

ABOUT THE AUTHOR

Nazia's dedication to help others in navigating their life's purpose as a life coach and social worker has allowed her to embrace her journey. To support her clients with their goals, Nazia believes it is crucial to connect with our 'human nature' to gain a deeper understanding of our needs that impact desired outcomes.

After serving diverse clients in various sectors of social services, Nazia recognized the importance of integrating cultural competency and utilizing strengths-based approaches when addressing each client's unique needs. Moreover, she advocates for occupational wellness or 'self-care' in health, human, and social service industries while collaborating with local community partners to raise awareness on important social topics in her podcast, Challenge Me 4 U.

Currently, Nazia is a social worker, MSW, at the Veteran's Administration Supportive Housing in Gainesville, FL., and a life coach at Wholistrans4mations.

Podcast: Challenge Me 4 U - Available on both Anchor or Spotify.

Website: wholistrans4mations.com

2

MICHELE SNEED, DSW, LGSW

THE UNNOTICED SCENERY

THERE WE SAT, two teenagers in the parking lot of Planned Parenthood. It had only been a few months since I met him and I was taking a pregnancy test at fifteen years old. I wondered what I had done. I felt the disappointment that would soon weigh heavily on my parents and the rest of the family. I was scared to death that he would take off running in the other direction. Ultimately, I was afraid that I would be alone, and that fear was overwhelming.

I was that teen girl who loved to push boundaries but would mask compliance along the way. At fifteen years old, I met this boy at the fair and then again at drivers' training and then a third time when I started high school. Our paths continued to cross, and very quickly young love took over. That day at Planned Parenthood when the positive test came back, I remember the car ride home was silent. Neither of us knew what to say or how we could take care of a child, and neither of us was comfortable with the decisions we had made that led us to this place. But the one thing I knew that day was that the dreams I had were now a distant memory. Surely I could forget about going to prom, college, and anything else that "normal" girls my age would experience, or at least that is what I believed.

I grew up in what I would have considered a very typical home. My parents were divorced when I was an infant and I lived with my mom, sister, and stepfather. My sister and I visited our dad and stepmother on the weekends, and I have a half-sister and half-brother who are quite a bit younger than I am. My parents, step-parents, siblings, and larger extended family are blessings to me. The value of family was instilled at a very early age by my maternal grandmother as one of the most influential people in my life. She was the glue that held all of her children and the twenty-some first cousins together. It wasn't unusual for us all to end up at grandma's house on the weekend picking teams for our softball tournament. At Christmas, my grandparents' house was filled to the brim with love, laughter, and a closeness that I did not appreciate until much later in life. Like any other family, we certainly had our share of issues that also helped shape me into the person I have become. These experiences and relationships drove me down the road to social work. Addiction, mental health, and domestic violence-plagued our family just as it does many others. When I was growing up, this didn't seem unusual because I didn't know anything else. As a social worker, I can now see that my protective factors outweighed the complicated and that the positive relationships I had within my family system helped grow me into the human being I am today.

The nine-plus months of the pregnancy were difficult. I was extremely ill in the first several months and was considered a high-risk pregnancy due to my age. I would find myself in the emergency room quite often due to dehydration. I switched to what I called a "pregnancy school" where other teen moms completed their academic coursework along with practical courses such as home economics, child development, budgeting, and other life skills that a new young mother needed to know. This is also where I met my first social worker. All of the girls in this program attended a support group one time per week where we discussed different topics. It typically entailed conversations about our relationships with the fathers and choosing between adoption or parenting our children. The social worker always amazed me. She was articulate and no-nonsense, yet enduring, and nonjudgmental. Most of all, she had a way of making us all feel comforted and safe at a time when things were so uncertain. She also ran a parent group where my partner was one of the only fathers-to-be who chose to attend.

The birth of my daughter gave me more than I ever expected. She gave me purpose and a drive I still can't fully explain. For the first time in a very long time, I felt the desire to accomplish things that I had thought were out of reach. She gave me the motivation to ensure that she had everything she ever needed. This did not come without obstacles. My daughter cried a lot during the first four months of her life. I would regularly be called out of class because my daughter was in daycare at the school and they could not stop her crying. They would tell me I had to come to get her because she was disrupting all of the other infants in the room. We would put her in the car seat on the washer/dryer or we would go for car rides and still, she would scream.

One night sticks out to me still to this day. I was a girl sitting in her teenage bedroom in the middle of the night with a screaming newborn. I had tried feeding her, changing her; we walked and we cried together. I was doing everything I could think of. I was weeping with her in my arms at the end of my bed when my mom walked into my bedroom, where teen posters and clothes were strewn about. She looked at me with empathy, gently took my daughter from my arms, and told me to get a couple of hours of sleep before school. At that moment, I realized that our choices not only affected me but two family systems in ways I could have never known. Our parents helped us tremendously and I believe their support was a main factor in the success we have had. They never took over the parenting role, but they made sure that we knew it was okay to be unsure, scared, and to ask for help.

I was waitressing at the time my daughter was born and continued to do so for many years. My son was born seven years after my daughter and we were delighted. We were in our early twenties and life seemed to be going very well. We had bought our first home and we felt grown. Looking back, I laugh at that statement like many probably would. The trials and tribulations are far too many to write about in this chapter. After my son was born, we had some critical crossroad moments occur in our life. This is when I decided I needed to move in a more positive direction. My decision to go back to school was unnerving. I had never been a "wonderful student". I was a social butterfly who had spent more time talking with friends than worrying about my academics. They didn't come easy for me but now I wonder how much I tried.

As young parents, my husband and I have always been ahead of those in our friendship circles due to the experience we gained in life early on. Our friends would come to us for advice, or we would find ourselves with people we barely knew who were pouring their hearts out to us. I thought about being a social worker or a psychology major because of these interactions, however I decided money was more important. I began school to be a dental hygienist. I honestly cannot tell you why I chose this field other than I thought it would be nice to work a four day work week and make decent money. After taking several classes in college, I quickly found myself rethinking this decision. I took sociology and psychology courses and I was mesmerized by people's feelings, their behaviors, their thoughts. I was taken aback by people's stories. After trudging through numerous science and math courses, I happily decided to switch my major to the social work program and was soon pregnant with my youngest daughter. She was born right before winter break and I was back in class immediately afterwards. I was determined that I was going to finish my degree. Never had I felt so "at home" as I did when I began courses in social work. It was almost as if the values were written for me. This feeling of belonging and connection to the profession has remained with me over the years.

The Transition into Child Welfare

Excitement, honor, and uncertainty. These are a few feelings I felt the day I earned my undergraduate social work degree. The excitement came from accomplishing this goal that had seemed impossible only a few years earlier. Excitement also came from the passion inside of me that was ready to explode as an agent of change. The social work field felt so "right" and I was honored to be part of a circle of people who genuinely cared about other humans. The shared values and purpose in social work were and continue to be what drives me in this work. I was uncertain of where my path in social work would lead me, but self-discovery, self-confidence, and the willingness to put myself in unfamiliar and uncomfortable positions has led me down a path I never would have imagined.

At the beginning of my career, I facilitated meetings with an amazing group of colleagues. This time was new and challenging, and when I met my second mentor in my career. She was a supervisor in the child welfare department. When she spoke, I was caught up in her words. She was so confident, intelligent, and strong, and she always had a kind word to share with me. I was part of a team that was following a family group decision-making model first used by the Maori people in New Zealand. Several philosophies came from this process: that families know one another best, families hold one another accountable, and that children should be kept within their family system whenever possible.

Although I loved facilitating meetings, I craved more. I wanted to talk with the families, listen to their stories, and understand the space they were in at this one moment in life.

Two years later, I got my wish and found myself in the position of a child protection ongoing social worker. There was nothing that could have completely prepared me for this work. I never imagined the lessons, skills, and humbleness it would teach me. The work forced me to remember the infinite importance of all people. I realized quickly that I could not change the world but I could join in their journey and nurture a working relationship at a time when their life struggles were getting in the way of them being able to be their best self.

During my first several weeks in this position, I would cry in the car on the way home. My worldview was small and I was overwhelmed by all of the feelings that were consuming my heart and mind. I grew up in a predominantly Caucasian community where I was able to not think about many of the situations my clients were experiencing. I had a family system that had many of the same issues that the families I worked with were experiencing yet my system offered protection. I remain humbled because there were many times in my life that I was simply one decision away from being someone else's client. My education prepared me for many things in social work but I don't believe there is any textbook that can fully prepare you for this profession. I witnessed firsthand the human suffering, fear, sadness, disconnection, and anger humans sometimes feel, yet I was amazed by the gift of resilience and love. This was not just a job, but a life-changing experience in my life.

After the initial culture shock, I was able to see the amazing attributes people bring to the table and how much kindness, transparency, and love we can bring to child welfare work. The clients I worked with taught me way more than I could have ever taught them. They were survivors, sometimes survivors of a system that complicated their life more than intended. I remember working with a mom who was struggling with addiction. The child was a beautiful five-year-old, and on my last visit, she looked at me and told me to wait. She went running upstairs to her bedroom and happily came running back down. She handed me a tiny blue bead. Initially, I thought she was just letting me know she had enjoyed our time together and wanted to give me a gift. As she handed me the bead, she told me that it was for me because I didn't have to worry about her anymore. My heart melted and I realized what she was trying to tell me was much bigger than either of us could have imagined. Some people think that working in child welfare or child protection is all stress, pain, and sleepless nights, but it's not. It is beautiful moments like these where you realize that simply genuinely caring about humans and working with them instead of against them can have great benefit. Another important experience that I have carried with me was when I had my first awakening about my white privilege and the idea of power. I was working with a Caucasian mother, an African American father, and their three children. I stopped by their home and was told I could walk to the backyard. In the backyard, there was a small table set up where the father and three of his friends were seated. I jovially and naively bounced happily up to the table and started introducing myself and offering to shake hands. The father of the children began introducing his friends when one stopped him and said, "Don't tell her my name!". It took me back. I wondered why I couldn't know his name. Did I do something wrong? Why is he scared of me, if I had never even met him before? Experiences like these deserve a book to themselves as people do not realize the knowledge that can be gained just from interactions in your environment if you open your mind to it.

Towards the end of my time in child protection, there were moments when I could identify trauma responses in my own actions. I would see a certain color of car that reminded me of a client and my body would react. I began to feel hopeless for the families I worked with. I would arrive home and not want to speak to my family because I was emotionally and mentally drained. I knew it was time to move on, but I thought moving on meant moving up the ladder and being further removed from direct client contact. I never imagined that I would ever leave the field of child welfare that had given me so much. I applied for supervisory positions several times but it never came to fruition. I was distraught and I felt underappreciated. My self-esteem took a hit, and for the first time in my professional career, I felt a bit lost. This ended up being the best thing that could have happened to me.

I sat reading a news article one day and saw that a local community college was looking to expand their human services program by partnering with a school to offer a four-year social work degree for local students. They were going to be holding a community meeting and I decided to make the drive to attend. I listened intently and was excited for our community as a whole. I spoke to the director of the human services program and shared my excitement. A month later, I saw they had posted a job for an Assistant Professor of Social Work. There was a fight inside as I contemplated whether or not I should apply. The teen mom dialogue in my head was still telling me I wasn't enough to do a job like this. I threw caution to the wind and decided to apply with no intention of hearing back. I did not tell anyone I had applied because I did not think I was smart enough to be a professor.

Six years later, I am currently the interim Chair of the Social Work Department and an Assistant Professor. Educating students has rejuvenated me. It is through the students that my passion was reignited and through an amazing group of colleagues who supported me and believed in me that I realized I was smart enough. I couldn't believe they were paying me to read books, stay current on research, and teach in a classroom full of excited soon-to-be social workers. Three years in, I decided that I needed to get my doctoral degree. The degree was not needed for my position but it became another personal goal that I needed to accomplish. It took me about three years, and writing the capstone and going through the editing process was harsh. Once again, my challenges in life led to my successes.

Life can be funny, the path we think we are destined to be on isn't always what we think and the lessons we learn are not always ones we even knew we needed. I started as a teen mom who had little hope that I could accomplish my dreams of working in child welfare with people who at differing degrees felt the same about their own life, to now sharing my knowledge and experiences with a new generation of social workers. My journey into and through social work is not done. I have more things I hope to accomplish and more things to learn. Reflecting on my journey has been emotional; it makes me proud, and it reminds me to stay grounded. I hope these experiences shared will instill excitement in those still seeking their professional path or at the early stages and hope to those that are feeling lost. Most of all, I hope my story reminds us to be patient, listen, and embrace all connections because the most important lessons I have learned have come from listening to others' stories.

Pearl of Wisdom

"Keep your eyes on your path ahead but don't forget to look at the scenery around you; you never know what purpose and connections you might see and where they will lead."

~ Michele Sneed

ABOUT THE AUTHOR

Michele Sneed, DSW, LGSW, Assistant Professor, Program Coordinator-Austin Campus, and Interim Social Work Department Chair started working at The College of St. Scholastica in the Social Work department in Fall 2016. Michele completed her Doctoral Degree in Social Work through Capella University. She obtained her MSW from the University of New England, her BSW degree from Winona State University. She also completed the Infant and early childhood mental health certificate program through the University of Minnesota and is trained in DC 0-5. She spent years of her career working within the child welfare system and in the recent past, Michele has worked as an individual and family therapist. Further experience has included the development of curriculum for community groups, facilitation, coordination of family meetings, authorship, and case management.

LinkedIn: linkedin.com/in/michele-s-ba4a62126

3
TEYA F. DAHLE, MSW, LICSW, IMH-E®(IV-C)

MY PATH

WHEN I THINK about where social work has led me, in the literal sense, I'm transported to many physical spaces; the expected spaces like office buildings, court rooms, schools, hospitals; the less expected like coffee shops, pet stores, laundromats, clothing stores, food shelf lines, living rooms, kitchens, vehicles; and the completely unexpected like closets (working on elevator fears), museums, inside seclusion rooms, barber shops, zoos, bathrooms (with families potty training toddlers), and barns (with birthing sheep).

A path is not solely about the destination. It requires a clearing and then a foundation to allow one to walk upon it comfortably.

Can one be born to be a social worker? From as far back as I can recall, I have been an observer and wonderer of others. I have early memories of peering out from behind my mother's legs as she greeted friends and strangers in our community, watching their facial expressions and listening to their expressive tones.

My social work path was forged by those at least two generations ago. My father worked as a social worker. He told stories of his work with immigrant families that preceded my birth. He worked in job placement with pregnant and parenting young moms and then for the State of Oregon. My earliest memories of his service involved visiting his office, frequent trips to the vending machine (with crisp $1 bills my father saved specifically for this), pretending to talk on his desk phone, drawing on huge pads of paper, pressing the green button on the copy machine, the glide of a brand-new pen, and hearing the sound of type-writers. If that wasn't the coolest measure of work success in the eyes of a young child, I could gauge the impact of his work by the smiles of former clients or coworkers that would approach us while out shopping. Though my mother was not a social worker, she has always led a life of service through education, music, and relating to all. My maternal grandparents too were educators and dedicated their lives to social justice. They all modeled that our voices and the voices of others were important, and that service could change the world.

I was introduced to home visiting as a preschooler. My mother, a kindergarten teacher, found value in visiting each of her student's homes and I was often by her side. She approached each home with a receptive smile and genuine interest. Her body was relaxed, which translated into a feeling of safety for me (with the exception of the one time we were attacked by a protective dog). The children would often run and greet my mother with laughter and a hug and the families would welcome us into their homes. There was usually a tour, the offer of homemade meals or treats, and a gracious "goodbye." As we would drive home in our VW bug, I would think about the unfamiliar accents or languages I heard, the new smells and flavors, the pride the family exhibited as my mother admired their home, their family, and the specific qualities she valued about their child. My mother never expressed negative judgment. She honored their lives and they in turn honored their relationship with her.

My foundational experiences were initially passive and that of an observer, until I was in the second grade. I learned about whales, the rarity of certain species, and about how many were moving toward extinction. I felt deeply about this, and certain that I, as a seven-year-old, could make a difference by creating a "Save the Whales" club. My mother gave her full support including providing paper for invitations and meeting notes and snacks and confirming with the parents of other invited club members that this was really a thing. I cannot recall what we actually did during club meetings, but my mother's affirmation that I could make an impact on the world is etched in my brain. Then, in the third grade, there was a child in my class who had bruises from her father. Having always felt safe with my parents, the thought of having a father hurt his child was confusing and upsetting. I remember an intense feeling of urgency and organizing a group of classmates to go to the teacher to inform her that our friend was being abused. Adults responded, but we were never given details. As eight-year-olds, we did not understand the complexity of familial abuse. We were certain that telling the teacher had saved our friend.

Some paths or portions of them may be bumpy with steep inclines. Others may be experienced as hazardous or may display warnings that ban certain types of travelers.

Like many, my path to social work was not paved solely with uplifting experiences. As a young child, three significant events occurred in close succession: my father was diagnosed with a chronic medical condition, requiring open-heart surgery; he experienced what I now understand as a single episode psychotic break; and he left our family for another. This marked the beginning of my worry he would die, the beginning of my mother parenting singly, and the beginning of weekends with Dad. I remember so vividly sitting by our front window on Saturdays, trying to guess exactly the number of cars that would pass until his car would turn into the driveway.

I have also had many experiences of feeling "othered" and moments where bias and racism were felt. I grew up in a very small rural farming town in Oregon with a very strong German Catholic heritage. It was a predominantly white community with a small percentage of families who identified as Mexican American. Most of my friends' roots in the community were generations deep. My parents met while attending college there; my father identifying as Filipino, from Hawaii, and my mother identifying as Euro-American from Oregon. Because of my race, my uncommon name, the fact that my parents were divorced (unlike all of my peers), my parents' progressive and liberal views, our practice of eating rice at most meals, and the use of "shoyu" as our primary condiment, along with our expressive ways of showing emotions, I felt different. My appearance led to many assuming I was Latina, and when they realized I was not, there was often a look of disappointment and sometimes a stronger disapproving expression if the person thought I was refusing to speak Spanish. Similarly, I'm assumed to be Hawaiian when I'm bound for Hawaii, but declared "Hapa Haole" when I arrive. Longing just to fit in, our family worked to embrace the cultural norms in our town. We wore dirndls during

Oktoberfest and picked berries in the summers. Beyond that, my strategy to feel accepted was proving my competence through hard work and at times, unhealthy perfectionism. My efforts and achievements earned respect from those who knew me but did not insulate me from microaggressions and bias from others.

A final experience that led to seeking a graduate clinical social work degree involved a family who was adapting to their child's diagnosis of autism. My psychology undergraduate internship (which would later become my employment) included providing a behavioral intervention that was effective in improving the child's functioning; however, beyond teaching strategies to parents, it did not address the non-finite grief and loss or the complex family challenges they were experiencing. I can recall a moment when a little boy was celebrating his birthday with our staff as a sort of practice for his scheduled party. I walked into the family's kitchen and discovered his mother, tears streaming down her cheeks. She had always imagined his fourth birthday differently and she was convinced they were running out of time to "cure" her son's autism. I was deeply moved and provided an empathic response but wished I could address her grief more fully. I felt certain there was more to know about helping young children and families and welcomed more schooling as part of my future.

Accommodating paths are developed with the rise and fall of the terrain in mind. Travelers of all abilities may walk safely.

"Have you thought of social work?" my psychology professor, Helena, asked, knowing my passion for social justice. I felt thankful for her recommendation as I discovered the mission—"...to enhance human well-being and help meet the basic human needs of all people, with particular attention to the needs and empowerment of people who are vulnerable, oppressed, and living in poverty" (National Association of Social Workers, 2021)—was congruent with my own. Before social work education, I had not heard the words "disenfranchised" or "oppressed" uttered or written so frequently; nor had I been encouraged to question the history printed in textbooks beyond thinking, "This book seems outdated, Reagan is no longer President." I had never been taught about the Civilization Fund Act and the historical practice of forced separation of Native American children from their parents (cultural genocide) despite growing up less than thirty miles from a boarding school. And before social work found me, considering race as a social construct imposed by those in power to maintain power and privilege had never crossed my mind. It felt affirming to be with fellow students and professors who shared my passion for social justice and often similar political views. And when views were not so similar, they knew how to respectfully wonder about our differing perspectives. We learned to be vulnerable together. We learned to embrace our imperfect family histories. I finally began to feel that my identities fit into my professional world.

Ideal paths have unobtrusive guides who walk beside or slightly ahead. Guides create guard rails, smooth the path around each step, spotlight bumps ahead, and steady the traveler if balance is lost. The guide's presence seems to magically regulate the atmosphere, making it tolerable during difficult and comfortable moments alike.

After graduate school in my first official social work position, I provided intensive in-home therapeutic services to families involved in the child protection system. I encountered countless unfamiliar and complex situations which left me wondering how I had been so unaware of the oppression faced by countless families. My awareness of judgements I had unconsciously formed was heightened. I was often flooded with intense feelings and questions: "How could a mother denounce one of three children and leave just that child on the doorstep of Child Protection?" "They think I am qualified as a new social worker to help this mother who is hallucinating, throwing glass, and threatening to kill herself?" "Did no one realize this child, who threatened his siblings with a gun, has autism and little awareness that his sisters actually thought he would shoot?" "Is it OK for an infant to crawl on the floor beside this dog poop? Isn't this parent going to pick him up?" "My heart aches for this family. Can't I just welcome them into my home?" I quickly recognized the importance of a skilled supervisor/mentor. My first social work supervisor, Vee, consistently made herself available. She provided a space to wonder together and to admit feelings of fear, frustration and sadness. After a lifetime of working to prove my competence, with Vee, I experienced it was safe to admit, "I'm not sure I know what to do!" In those moments when I was overcome by anxiety, Vee would relax into her chair, signaling her full presence. I could feel her calm, and in turn, my mind and body would also calm. She would truly hear me, she would affirm my competence and she would lead me to new possibilities. I soon began to recognize the parallels in the work. By holding Vee's calm in mind and returning to the felt experience of home-visiting with my mother, I could help families find calm, feel seen, and consider new possibilities.

I had worked for many years as a family therapist before I discovered a specialized path, Infant and Early Childhood Mental Health (IECMH). Just as I was drawn to the mission of social work, IECMH's foundational concepts resonated with me. IECMH is not just about knowledge of theory or rigid protocol; it is grounded in relationship, and to do the work requires conscious use of self. With Vee, I learned the value of a calming presence and the power of "being with," but would at times judge myself for not always harnessing the calm or not showing the "proper" emotional restraint. My emotions were not big enough to elicit a caretaking reaction from a client, but picture my huge smiles when parents shared a proud moment, wide eyes in the face of surprising information, and tears forming in the presence of another's tears. My body was also feeling the toll of years of absorbing the emotional experiences of others. I encountered Carol, a MN IECMH leader. There was and still is a familiarity about her presence that I cannot fully articulate. She so authentically painted pictures, communicated punctuation, and conveyed connection through her artful words, gestures and facial expressions. I could see myself in the way she approached the work and felt certain I could learn from Carol through reflective consultation/supervision. She helped me understand feelings as information, and through reflection, I was able to grow in my self-awareness. At times, the feelings were about my own life, but more often, the feelings provided clues about the families in my work. In one instance, I repeatedly expressed both comfortable and scared feelings while interacting with a specific parent. After first affirming my experience, Carol helped me learn this particular relational pattern could be indicative of an early history of parental hurt or harm. She would say, "It makes so much sense," and would continue to describe the pattern of relating as an adaptation to their history. Knowing this, I could adjust my approach in relating to this parent.

Carol also provided a protected space to discharge the cumulative stress I always tried so desperately to contain. In an effort to normalize my experience, Carol described and acted out the metaphor of an absorbent sponge. Much like an inflating balloon, she made a circle with her arms, extending them a bit further with each breath to represent the cumulative absorption of emotions and stress. When it appeared the "sponge" was full, Carol acted out the wringing of the sponge. I laughed and felt completely understood.

Social work, IECMH and reflective consultation/supervision alike, have reinforced an important foundational concept: the centrality of relationships. Many families who have little ones in need of services have had histories of less than desirable relationships, have difficulty with their own mental health, or are simply lacking helpful supports. I have had many moments in my career when I have felt ineffective and thought to myself, "We have been working together for months and, again, this parent threatens the child with foster care," or "Why can't the parent see and express joy in this baby?" During times when the work feels stuck and the path forward seems unclear, I am reminded that being consistent, predictable, regulating, and nurturing in my responses *is* the work. When a parent can experience these qualities in relation to me, they grow in their capacity and can engage in similar ways with their child. In all of my work, I hold central this quote by IECMH leaders Jeree Pawl and Maria St. John (1998): "Do unto others as you would have others do unto others" (p.7).

Notable paths offer opportunities to pause and reflect, to look about rather than straight ahead, to notice and navigate through and around barriers, and to take in the remarkable —thereby serving as a reminder as to why the path exists and continues.

Over the years, my social work path has provided opportunities to understand equity, diversity and inclusion in expanded and important ways. Through formal education, I learned about our nation's true history of oppression and racism. Through work experiences, I've been welcomed into the homes of diverse families who have shared their rituals, intimate stories of trauma, loss, and joy, and have trusted me to help their families regain regulation and connection. And through collegial relationships, I've felt a sense of belonging within my professional world. It wasn't until more recently, through IECMH studies, reflective supervision/consultation, and Diversity Informed Tenets mentorship that I allowed myself to pause and truly feel the impacts of racism. I've carried a lot of self-judgment about why it was hard for me to identify myself racially and why it had taken so long to embrace this part of me. I began allowing myself to think about countless experiences of feeling "othered." Many times, it was the looks that stung, not the words. Relating and blending required constant effort and hyper-awareness: "Is this a situation where I'm welcomed if perceived as white? Or would the person feel a stronger connection if it was known that I am a person of color?" I have had to remain aware of who and what I represent to a family, and their comfort or discomfort around that. Once, I drove a mother to a food shelf where she stood in line cursing and speaking obscenities about all of the immigrants and people of color in line taking *her* resources. I recall driving her home and feeling trapped and worried her hate may turn to me if she were to pause and notice my brown skin. In uplifting contrast, a little one adopted from China looked adoringly at me and said, "I have brown eyes, you have brown eyes. I have black hair, you have black hair. I'm Chinese, you're Chinese." Moments like the latter have helped me recognize I have a gift and a responsibility to use the privilege of being biracial in ways that can affirm and elevate others while staying true to my identity. Finally, I have begun to release myself from my own judgment through supportive relationships, and by remembering, "It makes so much sense." I had to adapt to feel safe.

When we walk the path of another, we see different perspectives and vantage points that illuminate the possible hazards and beauty. The sharing, the synchronous steps, and the felt experience are synergistic and strengthen the individual's path while also creating possibilities for shared and converging paths that continue infinitely.

Having walked my direct practice social work path for many years, I now have the privilege of walking beside IECMH, public health, child welfare/protection, child care and education providers through Reflective and Mental Health Consultation. This path spans individual, agency, school, county and national realms. I bring my authentic self along with all of the foundational experiences and teachings my path has illuminated over the years. Together, we create a protected, predictable space where the regulating presence of others can be felt; participants can organize their thinking and use feelings as information; we strive to remain curious about self, others, and the work; and we all can experience compassion, clarity, and "it makes so much sense"-moments. I feel that I'm honoring my path—past, present, and future

—and helping participants strengthen their own when they are able to "wring their sponge" of cumulative stress, self-doubt, and worries, and when they too are doing unto others as they would have others do unto others (Pawl & St. John, 1998).

Pearl of Wisdom

"In social work, the use of relationship is central. When a relationship feels challenging, consider the experiences we've lived, the identities we carry, and the hope we desire. Lean in while practicing self-awareness and compassion, and new paths forward will appear."

~ Teya F. Dahle

ABOUT THE AUTHOR

Teya Dahle, MSW, LICSW, IMH-E®IV-C – For more than 25 years, Teya has committed to "holding" the experiences of young children, their caregivers and community helpers through direct practice and reflective consultation/supervision in both rural and urban settings. Teya's formal education includes earning a Bachelor's degree in Psychology from Lewis and Clark College, a Master of Social Work degree from Portland State University, a Certificate in Infant and Early Childhood Mental Health (IECMH) from the University of Minnesota along with certification/rostering in several IECMH evidence-based practices. Currently, Teya manages the State of Minnesota's Early Childhood Mental Health Consultation System. She is an instructor for the University of Minnesota's IECMH program, has a private practice with a special focus on Infant and Early Childhood Mental Health, and is a mother of two. To all her work, Teya brings curiosity along with the Developmental Perspective, which is trauma informed and honoring of diversity.

4

CHERISH FIELDS, MSW, ED.S

UNEXPECTED DESTINY

"BEHIND EVERY SWEET SMILE, there is a bitter sadness that no one can see and feel." - Tupac Shakur

I remember the day I received a large manila envelope in the mail; it was thick and heavy. I tore it open, anxiously wondering if it was the information I had been waiting for. As I opened it, I quickly scanned over a letter informing me that enclosed was the case file I had requested from my time as a ward in Michigan's foster care system. You see, my life is unorthodox. I can't tell you about my family or my early years from memories. I only know the stories I have been told and the information written in my foster care case file.

My life's story begins during the era of crack cocaine in the United States. A young woman consumed with sex and drugs became a teenage mother to three babies before the age of twenty-one. My father was either in the streets or in jail. Due to my mother's lifestyle, he denied being my father. After child protective services received a complaint, we were removed from the location where my mother had abandoned us. Born to a prostitute and drug dealer, the odds were already stacked against me. This was the beginning of what would become a close acquaintance with the foster care system.

By the time I was five years old, I was finally adopted after multiple foster care placements. I was separated from my siblings since we had different fathers, and I was the last to find "permanency." Ironically, the one thing I vividly remember is my fifth birthday party, which was the last time I saw my siblings. Many individuals think that adoption automatically equates to a better life, but, honestly, my life got more complicated and chaotic. Being adopted was not a fairy tale. It was challenging for both my adoptive mother and me. Simply put, the scenario involved two individuals: one, a child with a significant trauma history, and the other, a single parent with considerable baggage herself that was inexperienced in dealing with trauma. We were always in conflict.

Shortly after adoption, life moved quickly. My adoptive mother decided to move us to Canada. However, it didn't work out; following that move, it felt like we continued to be "on the run." The moving stopped as my adoptive mother's health declined. When I was eleven years old, we lived in Georgia. Due to my adoptive mother's medical issues, our relationship became more strained than ever before. Our internal struggles were at odds and dominated the parent-child bond that we tried to form. Ultimately, our relationship turned abusive in contrast to the loving bond we sought to experience.

I can recall the day I found my adoptive mother on the floor of the apartment we shared. She had suffered a heart attack. Before that, she had a couple of strokes. Due to her illness, I assumed the role of caregiver. She never formally asked me to carry out this task, but the responsibility fell on me since it was just the two of us. After that, we pretty much lived in the hospital or with strangers. My adoptive mother struggled to care for us, but eventually, I ended up mainly caring for her. And in the process, I lost my childhood.

For a brief moment, I spent time in juvie for running away from "home." I was determined to get away from the chaos I experienced there. Thankfully, the judge decided I would be placed in foster care after finding my adoptive mother was no longer in the state and no relatives came forward willing to care for me. Instead of disappointment, I was relieved. I needed a better situation. However, I didn't know that it would soon become worse. After multiple failed placements, I quickly became the blame for the disruptions at each placement. "She is the problem," they would say. Maybe I was. The truth is, I had the audacity to speak out about the mistreatment I and other children experienced in foster care. Kids like me were often forced to endure cruelty, microaggressions, unsavory treatment, and downright abusive situations simply because there were no other options. I would often argue with workers to try and get them to understand our plight, but I would go unheard. I suppose it was easier for them to turn a deaf ear since the resources were few and options were non-existent for teenagers. It was well known that you were not wanted if you were a teenager in care.

One day, as I sat in the waiting area at the Department of Family and Children Services (DFACS) office, I observed a woman sitting across the room. She had a deep but friendly southern dialect. I decided to boldly ask her what she was doing at the office. She told me that she was a foster parent waiting for a little boy in her care. I inquired if she fostered teens. She replied, saying she had never taken them before. I, of course, surveyed her a bit more. After hearing she was active in the church, which interested me, I quickly asked if she would consider me. She agreed to try an overnight visit. With excitement, I went to share the news with my caseworker. I had found my own placement.

After a couple of years in foster care and the state pushing their agenda to reunify me with my adoptive mother, her battle with several lifelong illnesses ended with her death. She left this world and left me at four-teen years old–and I would finish growing up in the foster care system.

In dealing with the passing of my adoptive mother, the family I advo-cated to stay with did not work out. I lived there long enough for them to initiate the adoption process, but I ended up leaving before it was finalized. Behind those closed doors, I endured emotional and sexual abuse. After that family, I didn't have much trust in the system. The options provided to me seemed to cause more damage instead of the safety I longed for. Foster homes were not a good fit for me. After that, I ended up spending a few years in residential placement where I actu-ally excelled. My grades were the highest they had ever been. I joined sports teams, held a part-time job, and became involved in social clubs.

By the time I turned fifteen, my life was uprooted again. I left Georgia to move back to Michigan. I hesitantly gave adoption another try but again it resulted in disappointment. At this point, I scrambled to keep everything I had worked hard for together, especially in school. In my mind, the system couldn't take my education. I rallied letters of support from teachers, school leadership, and fellow classmates to aid me and advocate for my stay in Michigan so that I could graduate from high school. However, I was still a ward of Georgia's foster care system. Since the adoption did not work out and there was no hope of reconciliation, I would have to return to Georgia. For me, that was not an option I was willing to settle for.

At that point in my life, I had attended fourteen different schools and was in my fifth high school. I couldn't afford another move as a senior. I spoke to my case managers, called supervisors, and relentlessly pleaded my case until I could get an answer. I didn't have a relationship with any of my workers. They were constantly changing, so I knew never to get comfortable with them. At the time, I considered them part of the cruel system that made my life a living hell. Thankfully, with the support of friends, I worked up the courage to apply to college, which was not in my original plan. I had some exposure to the idea, but I would only act interested. As a foster kid, I didn't see myself in college. I didn't think that was a place for someone like me.

I always had the dream of becoming a hair salon owner. Luckily, before decisions were made, I received multiple acceptance letters from colleges, one of which was the University of Michigan-Ann Arbor. I was awarded a full-ride scholarship. Sharing this news with the state, I was allowed to stay in Michigan. A friend asked an involved parent at our school if she would allow me to stay with her until I went off to college. She accepted, and I was grateful. Things were starting to settle.

During my college years, an emptiness befell me. I thought I had made it. But as I watched other students go home for the holidays or call home to share their achievements, they served as reminders that I did not have anyone. I had successfully climbed a mountain but had no one to share my achievements with. I felt alone, which left me wondering about my birth family. I decided to search for them. That manila envelope I received in the mail held all the information available about my early childhood and gave me a starting point to find my birth mother. As I entered her name into the state prisoner tracking system online, I soon learned that she was closer than I imagined. The first time I met my birth mother was in the cold confines of a prison visiting room. Never meeting before that moment, and with no pictures to reference or memories to recall, I had a hard time accepting that we were related, let alone that she was the woman who gave birth to me. There was a heavy exchange of questions and answers in that room that would challenge me, how I viewed myself, and what I would be as I looked ahead to my future.

In my continued college studies, I became more interested in social systems. I always chose to write my papers about my foster care experience because that was the only experience I knew. As I continued to visit the prison, I explored the criminal justice system and the possibility of becoming an attorney. I cultivated this passion for advocating for others who were disadvantaged and unjustly treated. I felt a sense of connection to this experience. However, as I got to know my birth mother, this connection to foster care became stronger.

I continued to live in survival mode, and my spirit was tired. I was unsure if I would make it to graduation due to mental and emotional exhaustion. I knew that giving up would equate to homelessness and failure. I had no safety nets outside of what college supplied me. I was dependent on it, and I had to make it work. I decided not to let the conditions of my life rule me. I chose myself. I developed a determination that stemmed from this mix of anger and sadness I held within. I had to prove the system wrong and everyone who believed anything negative about me. It gave me the drive I needed.

In my final year of undergrad, I had this constant urge to create a space where other kids could realize they had the ability and opportunity to attend college, just as I did. I wanted to show the world that kids placed in foster care have more potential than limitations. They were worth the investment of a future, and so it began; I sent emails and solicited funds to host a conference, specifically for teens in foster care. The support was overwhelming. With the University of Michigan as my biggest backer, I put on the *Rising Above the Odds Against Me* Youth Conference. For over 100 adolescents, it was their first-time stepping foot on a college campus and hearing from someone who had a similar experience as them. In my journey, I had no one to look up to. I didn't realize until that event how much it was needed. In sharing my story, I empowered others to share their voice. I wanted to create an opportunity for them to feel heard and valued. Afterwards, attendees shared feedback that the conference saved their life from the thoughts of suicide and self-harm, and now they felt inspired to fight for their future. I continued to hold events for three years at various campuses, but the influence of child welfare politics turned me off and limitations and restrictions slowly diminished my vision. I decided the conference had run its course as my life moved into a new season and onto my professional path.

Symbolically fitting, I finally became a Wolverine as a graduate of the University of Michigan. Not only did I graduate from college, but I graduated from the top public university in the country. I was a part of less than 3% of foster youth to accomplish this feat. I couldn't believe it myself! This made me a first-generation college graduate. After the emotions of my accomplishments began to fade, I found myself realizing I needed to figure out what was next. After talking to some friends, I was told that the University of Michigan School of Social Work had extended its application deadline that year, which rarely happened. So, I applied! I never had the goal to become a social worker, but I figured why not try. I did know that I wanted to help youth. I just wasn't sure which avenue I would take. To my surprise, I was accepted; and what's more, it was an almost immediate response.

I received a scholarship to become a child welfare scholar. It seemed like destiny unfolded before me. I became enthralled in gaining a deeper understanding of the child welfare system. In fact, I had fallen in love! Graduate school was captivating and social work had my heart.

After grad school, I started work in juvenile delinquency programs, but quickly learned it was not for me. I learned about the cross-over between foster care and juvenile justice youth. However, my heart pulled me towards child welfare. I got a job in the private sector of social service that allowed me to work in various direct practice roles in foster care. An opportunity arose for me to work in residential for a small non-profit in Detroit. From there, I grew professionally into leadership roles, becoming an executive leader. As I evolved, so did my mission. It morphed from having a direct impact on youth and families to improving the quality of programs and services they experienced. I grew tired of the disappointments and unnecessary barriers of the system, many of which replicated issues from what I experienced growing up. It was clear the system had not changed but had instead adapted new words to reference. After witnessing the system become its own enemy and cause harm to children rather than support them, it solidified that a real change was needed. In 2019, I started a podcast called "Child Welfare Leaders." The podcast was born out of frustration with the complacency in child welfare. I needed a space where voices could be heard to inspire others to lead change against the status quo. It was my calling to advocate for being the change we need to see in the system.

"We wouldn't ask why a rose that grew from the concrete had damaged petals; in turn, we would all celebrate its tenacity, we would all love its will to reach the sun, well, we are the roses, this is the concrete, and these are my damaged petals, don't ask me why, thank god, and ask me how"

- Tupac Shakur

My experiences gave me an understanding of how my life's story had significance in my work. At certain tables in child welfare, I have often felt that my "lived experience" was not welcomed or respected at the level it should have been and instead has been viewed as a threat to the conversations about change. However, my life's events are what led me to social work. After becoming a foster parent for a few years, I learned that poor treatment is not solely experienced by the child. I noticed that the system has a way of conditioning people. I found that forces at work within the system outweigh the influence of those working to change the system. I know this work personally; coupled with over ten years of professional experience, I have been a product of how it feels. Now I understand the brokenness within the child welfare system. This knowledge led me to the next chapter of what I call "social workprenuerism." As a social worker building a business, I am focusing on solutions that change the experiences within child welfare and challenge the status quo by empowering, equipping, and leading individuals and professionals beyond the system's limitations. I've also learned that some changes have to happen outside the system.

Reflecting on my upbringing, my goals then were simply to survive. Over time, my goals evolved. It all started from the deep need to survive and moved in a natural progression that led me to an *unexpected destiny*. I never considered social work because of its connection to foster care, which I had tried to avoid. My life was filled with many negative experiences with workers. There were a few good ones, but there was already an excellent social worker in me, as you have read in my story. Now, I am a proud activist for child welfare change. One who went from living within the system and surviving it to serving in and being a part of leading child welfare change. As for where social work led me, it led me to a purpose greater than the conditions of my life.

Pearl of Wisdom
"Life will try to limit you; use limitations not to be limited, but to become a limited edition of everything you are destined to be."
~ Cherish Fields

ABOUT THE AUTHOR

Cherish Fields is challenging the status quo. From being a product of foster care to becoming a Child Welfare Leader and sought-after speaker, she hosts a podcast called Child Welfare Leaders. Cherish is a trained MSW obtaining her education from University of Michigan. She has dedicated her career to improving the experience of those who encounter the child welfare system and creating generational impact. Her work on the importance of relationships was published in the Michigan Social Work and Social Justice Journal in 2011. In 2015, she was honored with the House of Providence Survivor Award which in 2021 became the "Cherish Fields Survivor Award". She is a recipient of the Survivor Foundation Social Worker of the Year Award, and 2019 Dedicated & Deserving Social Worker Award that was featured in the Social Worker Today magazine. Outside of work, she is blessed to be happily married with two children.

Podcast: anchor.fm/cherishfields-msw
Instagram: @cherishfields_MSW
LinkedIn: linkedin.com/in/cherish-fields-msw-ed-s-17482411/

5

ELIZABETH WENDEL, MSW, LSW

LETTERS OF R.E.S.I.L.I.E.N.C.E.

I HAVE COMPLETED a Master's in Social Work, read thousands of pages from thousands of books, articles, and research papers, and am grateful to the many teachers, co-workers, authors, and personal supports who helped me do it. The perspective I present here, however, was learned much earlier in my life, before all the books, and is foundational to who I am as a person and a professional. I begin here because I cannot tell you where social work may lead *you* but hope that my own personal example of looking back at my life and reflecting on concepts that may seem familiar can help you identify new toolsets and bolster old ones along your own journey.

As I reflect on my own personhood and my education in and out of the classroom, I find a few core ideas define who I am in practice. One, forged out of a deep understanding of personal struggles, has become a driving force of my own social work aspirations: <u>resilience is built</u>.

It is well understood that a traumatic experience can change someone's life. A positive experience can have an equal and measurable impact to the long-term well-being of any human. The most powerful positive experiences are buffering, protective, and nurturing moments that sometimes follow trauma. This can take the form of a simple moment, offering support, listening, a hello, a hug. It can take the form of many nurturing experiences strung together in the days, weeks, and months following. At times, these moments come from people we love and hold dear in our daily life. Other times, they may come from a relative stranger or social worker who is in our life for just a short time. Each of us can offer these experiences, model these experiences, and support others and *systems* to build these experiences for every person. Within the work that we do, wisdom may come from simply recognizing this connective tissue that recovers us is the core of who we are as human beings; incredible resilience built from the relationships that nurture, re-center, and unconditionally love before, during, and after trauma are world changing.

In the following pages, I offer letters written to reflect on key life-altering times in my life. These letters are not an admiration or celebration of the trauma. Instead, they are an honoring of the positive experiences that came after: the undoubtedly simple positive moments that changed my life and hold more power than trauma or suffering itself. These are honor letters to the resilience building moments and the people who made them. These have shaped who I am in my understanding of resilience-building all around us.

A Letter to My Sister

Having a sister is unlike anything else in the world; it is constant in a way few relationships are. I am thankful to have you as my older sister. As kids, we played together, set up intricate worlds for our Barbies, and choreographed cool dance moves as Whitney Houston sang "I Wanna Dance with Somebody." I am so grateful for those memories. As many stories are, this one we hold together would be incomplete without acknowledgement of the deep suffering endured during our early years. The abuse you experienced left you with a deep and confusing wound. No child should ever be harmed the way you were, and as your sister I know the impact it left in its wake.

In your teen years, your suffering had become so immense it was unbearable. I know you felt alone, unable to put words to the experiences you had endured. Although the threat was physically gone, the experience remained. We hold in our bodies and minds the experience and its residual havoc on our nervous systems long after the trauma has ended. This was true for you, as it is for so many people who endure this type of trauma.

"Take what you've learned and use that to see the world differently. You use your pain and transform it to power and help other people. I think of the most transformative people I've ever known, every single one of them had personal pain and traumatic experience that was a core element of who they became." – Dr. Bruce Perry, *What Happened to You?*

You couldn't escape the thoughts, words, and feelings that bombarded you. Your voice disappeared to keep the suffering hidden away; your incredibly powerful mind tried to protect you from a violation it could not make sense of. In your deepest suffering, you tried to take your own life. I am thankful now and always that you survived. I have sometimes wished for a magic wand to undo the horrible things you endured. Instead, we stood together. The suffering you carried and the worry I felt for you has evolved into something much more powerful: hope.

The suicide attempt was a beginning, a moment of opportunity, to embark upon the arduous process of putting words, feelings, and movement to the trauma and to untangle what had happened to you from who you were, are and would become. That work happened day by day. And it did happen. You emerged from that space over time to become something remarkable—a human being who knows a unique suffering in a way that no one ever should but so many do. For me, you became a beacon of strength, wisdom, and most importantly, hope.

In addition to being a sister, daughter, mother, wife, and friend, you now spend your days welcoming refugees into our home city. You are with people during some of the most terrifying, confusing, and life-changing moments of their lives. You stand with people. You know that the simple act of holding hope for people as they are welcomed in can create even a small moment of comfort, a port in the storm. That port for some makes all the difference.

I think about what you built from your own traumatic experiences and what you have since given to so many others. What was once suffering is now wisdom, strength, and courage to be hopeful for so many around you.

You know what justice-doing and hope-giving look like. It is in your wise DNA. It is shared with so many people who have been touched by your time and energy and courage. Your willingness to struggle yourself with thoughts, and feelings, and despair, and hope led you to this place, and it is exactly where you are meant to be. You hold hope for others, even when others cannot hold it for themselves.

You transformed your pain into power. You are a living example of what it means to deeply know and look at your own suffering and use it for the betterment of the world around you. Even if you cannot take away the suffering of the world, it is made better by your simple holding hope for and standing with those around you. This is a beautiful example of resilience: built, internalized, and shared.

47

A Letter to My Mom

Occasionally, someone says to me, "You are so much like your mother." There is no greater compliment in the world. In fact, as a child, I called you "The Queen Mother of All the World." You were then, and you are now.

"Every child needs at least one adult who is irrationally crazy about him or her." – Urie Bronfenbrenner

I cannot think of a better way to learn about social work than having a mother who is a social worker. Growing up, you were brilliant at shielding us from the worries of your work, and you were equally brilliant at modeling and instilling in us the most essential knowledge of what it means to be a good human in the world: to hold hope for others, to know in your gut what's right. All people deserve love. This is not a complicated thing. In a world where so many systems and spaces have made suffering and its doing or undoing incredibly complicated, you reminded me of a simple beginning: sit with people, listen, and be beside them in their grief, worry, fear, hope, love, joy, confusion. When we share in this, even just us two, it is less to carry. When I share that with others, it is less to carry. I learned this from you.

As a little girl, the worries of life and what was happening were only a part of the story. Out of a deep respect for all who are mothers, I acknowledge that all mothers worry. Some live in places or deal with things that lead to a deep aching worry no one should ever have to feel. You, mom, feel the world and its worries. No matter how long that worries list was, you made even the most daily tasks a joyous adventure.

Whatever we were doing, no matter how mundane or common, it was an adventure. At the grocery store, we'd jet off on a mission to find a mystery ingredient. On afternoons spent cleaning the house, I'd come running in to show you how much dust I'd captured on my rag. When guests were coming to visit, we pulled at the chalk to draw a welcome mural on the sidewalk. You loved us through every moment of every normal part of the day, and through the hard parts of some incredibly awful days. You made your love for us crystal clear in every moment. You buffered us with your love.

Buffering is not the absence of adversity; instead, it is the presence of key relationships of love in our lives that help bring us back to balance, help us digest and understand adversity, and build resilience to bring us back to balance more quickly in adversity yet to come. Each dose of buffering builds us stronger. Buffering happens in everyday moments, everyday life. I cannot count the thousands of moments you have done this for me, for my sister, for so many families in the work you did. To try and count these moments of love would be impossible, so I won't even try. I am who I am because of them; I understand how important they are for every person because of you.

Those doses of love were essential for me, and they are essential for every person in the world. In our work, we must remember we can give that love and we can simply recognize its importance and make it a part of our work to ensure everyone has access to that love every day. These doses build resilience.

A Letter to My Dad

"When you cannot see the light, I will sit with you in the dark." - Unknown

"You look like your dad." There is nothing that makes me laugh more quickly. I laugh because you adopted us, and so biologically and genetically speaking, it is scientifically unlikely I look like you. Upon further evaluation though, I wonder if I look like you because I've picked up your mannerisms, your sayings, your facial expressions, and, I hope, your wisdom about people in the world.

During what I call my middle growing up years, we lived on a beautiful mountain. There were trees on three sides, and it was a quiet place. The chaos of life meant the insides of our collective spirits did not often match the outside space we lived in, but there was a calm there.

One afternoon, you hung up a hammock outside. It was woven blue and hung exactly between two trees where you had installed eye hooks to keep it secure. I swung. And swung and swung and swung. With my trusty discman at my side (and excellent music, thank you Backstreet Boys), I would swing for hours. I would sing as I felt the breeze go by as I swung on the blue hammock.

"She's swinging a lot," my mom would say to you. "It's good for her," you would reply.

The wisdom here is a deep one. In a time where there was so much unknown, so much worry about my sister, about what had happened when we were younger, about what would happen next, you knew the importance of this swinging. For me, it was an escape; a regulation of my body and mind in concert together; a quiet I didn't know I needed.

I spent so many hours swinging on that hammock that I wore down the metal of the eye hooks that fixed it to each tree. Once every few months, I would go outside to my

swinging spot and find that new hooks had miraculously appeared. No words, no talking, just new hooks to make sure I could continue swinging without falling. Those hooks were a simple example of the care you gave, every day, without fail. It made all the difference.

I am grateful for that hammock, and for you hanging it and replacing its hooks. You knew how to create calm in the chaos. You knew what I needed. Literal and figurative care. No matter what, I wouldn't fall. In my work now, I remember that healing happens in the body and the brain as one as a supersystem. Sometimes, before a long conversation or untangling of trauma, swinging in a hammock is required. This is resilience built from care.

A Letter to Myself

At 29 years old, I went blind in one eye. At first, no one knew what was happening. I sat in a meeting, and within seconds, I couldn't see. I was afraid.

And then my trusty brain kicked in. "It's nothing," I thought. Just to be safe, I went to see a doctor that afternoon, by which time the blindness had subsided. "Let's get it checked, just in case." I made an appointment for the following Monday.

"Healing is messy and human and gut-wrenching and hilarious. It is not a precise science." – Father Greg Boyle

I made it through the weekend, where another bout of temporary blindness had occurred. By Monday night, I was sitting in a hospital room following a brain scan, waiting. I had re-dressed and was ready to go home. Instead, I was instructed to wait. A few more doctors filed in. "There is a black space in your brain scan. It could be a tumor, a massive viral infection, or a stroke. We just don't know." I spent the coming days on the neurology floor of the hospital being poked and prodded and tested. Even when I was permitted to go home, we didn't have an answer about what was happening.

Following many more outpatient tests, we had a diagnosis. I had a stroke at age 29. As I tell this story, I remember the fear. Almost immediately though, something else floods my system: the doses of hope, care and love I got in those moments and the many months following. Amazing doctors and nurses walked me through the medical conversation about healing. And it was my loved ones, my incredible network of support, who spent time with me in the hospital, laughing, joking, talking, and crying together, that helped me heal.

The initial worry that I had a stroke at 29 quickly gave way to a practical reality: I was lucky. I had a stroke with no visible aftermath. I needed to live my life. I used the hope, care, and love my family and friends offered to get back to doing all the things that mattered to me, including my work. As it turned out, all the foundational things I learned from the three people I wrote to here were still with me. They were still as clear as ever. Healing didn't happen in the hospital room; it happened in my life, with the people I loved walking beside me.

These letters I share here were born from letters I wrote to many loved ones during the early parts of my stroke, when I didn't know what was going to happen or how sick I might be. Some of my words are borrowed from the things I know to be most true in my scariest moments and ones I hope we hold at our center in the work we do with others: hope, care, love, and healing.

I come to you humbled by time and experience but confident in my journey to resilience. These early learnings have been proven time and time again through academic and professional practice; proven from the experience of standing with and in support of children and their families; proven from the testimony of practicing professionals and survivors alike. Resilience is built and nurtured by the unconditional relationships that support you in navigating and growing from trauma or experience. These letters honor the resilience built through foundational relationships; they are made of the simple beginnings of my worldview and the hope I hold within it.

Resilience is not the absence of suffering, as much as we might wish that for the people we love. Instead, resilience is the ability to recover through and become wise from that suffering. My hope for our work is to model an intentionality about every interaction: how can resilience be built here? How can this person's key relationships be found, nurtured, or supported by me as a professional?

My journey in social work will be different from yours, but perhaps highlighting our capacity to recognize resilience is built by a village of people and experiences rather than a superpower skill. That village is the superpower. Take any opportunity to reflect on experiences to gently nudge your own journey in this precious and precipitous path. I am confident you will see just how much power and knowledge you hold and the gift they can be for the world.

Pearl of Wisdom

"Resilience is not the grieving of trauma; it is the power we draw from relationships to grow from it."

~ Elizabeth Wendel

ABOUT THE AUTHOR

"It is not how many people we find; it is what we do with the people we find." Elizabeth, MSW, LSW is a model co-author, subject matter expert, and advocate of **Family Finding, Family Seeing** work across the globe. Her consulting, writing, teaching, and strategic support have taken her to work in Australia and New Zealand, Canada, the United States, various parts of Central and South America as well as Western Europe.

Elizabeth's original focus was within the American foster care system, where her program work in Family Finding allowed her a lens into advocacy for family connection and well-being at the clinical, as well as policy and funding levels. Elizabeth now continues that expertise and examination through work with government systems, private organizations and coalitions, and healthcare companies working with children and adults.

For each person on this planet, the reality we must hold fast to: more love, not less. Elizabeth's work can be found via social media and on her website.

Website: familyfinding.org

6

GILBERT DOMALLY, M.A., LGSW

A REFLECTIVE JOURNEY TOWARDS A PROFESSION

"It doesn't matter what you do; you are going to be a social worker." I heard these words in my heart while standing before a jobs bulletin board in the Olmsted County Government Center in Rochester, Minnesota over twenty years ago. At the time, I was a young husband and father working several other jobs to make ends meet. I was tired a lot, but for the most part I didn't mind the jobs and associated work since they served the purpose of providing for my family. Yet, I did have a sense that these jobs were not meant to be my destination. I believed there was a professional track that could allow me to adequately provide for my family while doing something that was aligned with who I am as a person in terms of my temperament, natural aptitudes, interests, skills, and abilities. However, there were a few things that challenged my access to the right track for me, which I know now to be social work.

Though I heard those words, I didn't really understand what they meant or how to apply them to my life because I had very limited exposure to the social work profession. While attending the University of Nebraska Omaha as a family science major, I had once heard my academic advisor mention that my major was related to social work, but we didn't have an in-depth discussion about it. I also had a friend that was completing a social work degree, but it wasn't clear to me what kind of work he intended to do with his degree. The next barrier, though I didn't see it as a barrier, was my perspective on the earnings potential for social workers after doing some research. When I looked at social work job wages and compared them to the wages of jobs in other fields, I thought, "I can't make enough money to support my family doing social work." It wasn't true, but it's what I believed at the time.

The last and perhaps greatest challenge to my engagement in the profession of social work was the lack of deep, personal exploration and reflection.

"The families that produce social workers are not atypical of the general population; they represent every point on the social and developmental continuum" (Lackie, 1983). My family of origin was certainly "…not atypical of the general population….". It was very typical, with its share of strengths, protective and complicating factors which shaped my intrapersonal and interpersonal development in ways that were preparing me for the world of social work.

I am a part of a very large and complex family system; I am the fifth child of my mother's eight children and the third child of my biological father's five children. Despite the large and complex nature of my family system, it was a great holding environment for learning the power of attachment in developing resilience. Because of my birth order, I had a unique opportunity to observe and experience my mother develop as she responded to the challenges of raising her children in the context of broken relationships with their fathers. My mother entered parenthood as a teenage mother of twins, and was twenty-four when she gave birth to me. I remember as a small child recognizing that life was hard for her at times. Yet, my mother maintained an interesting presence about her that exuded a calmness and confidence that she would get through whatever life presented her way, and she conveyed that same calmness and confidence to me.

In fact, up until I was about eleven years old, I repeatedly heard my mother say, "I know you can do it because you are my son!" It really didn't matter what the situation was, her perspective and expectation of me was that I had what it took to be successful and get through it. She was my greatest cheerleader and communicated that, if by some chance I didn't succeed, her belief in me would not change. I think my mother's confidence in me stemmed from her personal experiences effectively navigating life's trials. Through my secure attachment with my mother, I learned how to be resilient, engage people in a positive manner, and convey a belief in the ability of others to persevere through life's challenges, especially when someone has hope for them.

"Research suggests that children with involved and engaged fathers tend to have more positive outcomes relative to physical, cognitive, and social emotional health" (Campbell et. al, 2015). I am the child of three fathers. One who gave me life, another who gave me a name, and one that raised me and greatly influenced my view of masculinity and the importance of fatherhood. I am grateful for each of my fathers, but for the purpose of this chapter, I will focus on the father who raised me and his contributions to my preparation for social work.

Though not a perfect man, my father was a strong and protective factor in my life. My father is a tall, African American, physically imposing, articulate Marine with a quiet yet commanding presence. He enjoyed being a Marine, exercising, watching football, basketball, boxing, Westerns, Perry Mason, and fishing. My father is also comfortable with a wrench in his hand. If I were to end the description of my father at the previous sentence, one might be tempted to make certain assumptions about him and the ways that he shaped my development that would be woefully inaccurate and incomplete.

Though a cisgendered, heterosexual male, my father was not a man that allowed himself to be bound by male stereotypes which contributed to a largely egalitarian home environment. When it came to parenting, my father was just as involved as my mother. My father provided instruction, discipline, structure, and an understanding of the importance of education. I remember my father spending entire weekends teaching me math and reviewing my homework and report cards. There was a time when my mother was sick and hospitalized for an extended period, during which he cooked, baked, did hair, and whatever else my younger siblings and I needed. On another occasion, he performed the same duties while demonstrating that it was okay to receive help when he needed it; he allowed me to understand the power and benefits of community in fostering resilience.

When I was eleven years old, due to a series of unfortunate and life-changing events, my father found himself caring for me and my three youngest siblings by himself. My sisters were eight and one years old and my youngest brother was almost five. It was a very destabilizing and hard time for our family as we were already a family in transition when the events occurred. My father had just completed his military obligation and we had relocated to South Florida where we were in the process of re-establishing ourselves as a civilian family. Nevertheless, my father took to the task of taking care of and providing for me and my siblings. However, unlike the other times when he cared for us for relatively brief periods of time, he enlisted help.

We lived with my paternal grandparents, one of my aunts and a couple of my uncles that lived with us on and off for the most part until I graduated from high school. My siblings and I went from being a part of a traditional military household with two primary caregivers to being a part of a civilian, multi-generational family system in a new city with a culture dramatically different than what we were used to. It reminds me of Rueben Hill's "ABC-X Model of family stress and coping…a framework for analyzing the relationship between stressful events and crises with families"(Rosino, 2016) and McCubbin and Patterson's (1983) adaptation of the model, the Double ABC-X Model. Instead of one event or stressor, the "A" part of the model, taxing our family's resources—the "B" part of the model—we had several stressful events that occurred within the same time frame. Each member of the family held the perception, the "C" part of the model, that the events were negative for our family and that we were in a "X" crisis that would likely alter our family for the foreseeable future.

In response to the various stressors and ensuing crisis, our extended family endeavored to fill in the gaps. While my father worked, my grandparents, aunt, and uncles to a lesser extent provided us with care and supervision. Living in this kind of arrangement served to strengthen some of the values that I had learned when my nuclear family was intact. Although I am not an eldest child, I was raised as an eldest child and elder grandchild. Under the watchful eyes of my grandparents, I helped with the dishes, vacuumed, swept, cut grass, did laundry, and ran errands. I also assisted with caring for my younger siblings. It wasn't always fun or enjoyable, but we had a roof over our heads, food to eat, clean clothes to wear (though never name brand), shoes on our feet and people with clear expectations for us. We were poor and rich at the same time: poor in terms of financial resources and possessions but rich in terms of care, discipline, and clear expecta-tions. Living in a large economically poor, multi-generational family system as result of crisis created many opportunities to appreciate having the basics, develop a strong work ethic, patience, humility, and empathy for people in less fortunate circumstances.

I was not aware of it at the time, but the experiences I had in my paternal family, both good and not so good, were educating me for a career in social work and specifically child welfare. I had received a firsthand education on strengths/protective factors, complicating factors, and resilience. I was exposed to the fact that families are quite capable of effectively raising children despite trauma and living in difficult circumstances; this turned out to be a necessary lesson that could only be enhanced by academic exposure.

Education

As of the writing of this chapter, I have never completed a bachelor's or Masters of Social Work program. When I began college in the early to mid-90's, I wasn't clear what profession I would pursue. I attended Rochester Community College in Rochester, Minnesota where I considered athletic training because I enjoyed sports and was a wrestler in college. However, a few brushes with general science classes helped me understand that this might not be a good idea. I took a career orientation class where I completed a Strong Interest Inventory Test which suggested that I consider human service careers, ministry, or law enforcement. Yet, I still didn't have a clear direction. So, rather than intentionally pursue a course that would lead to training for a specific profession, I took classes to remain eligible to compete in wrestling and completed an associate degree in two years which would allow me to transfer most of my credits to a four-year university.

I didn't have a focus, but I did excel in English and social science classes. After two years at Rochester Community College, I transferred to the University of Nebraska Omaha on an athletic scholarship where I learned about a major called Family Science. My academic advisor shared with me that it was closely related to social work. It seemed to fit my interests, so I began to pursue the major, but left school to return to Minnesota prior to completing the degree.

Upon my return to Minnesota, I found out that the nearest school to Rochester with a family science program was the University of Minnesota. Without a scholarship and no other sources of financial assistance apart from student loans, I didn't see how I could afford to complete the degree. So, I took a break from school, worked, and eventually joined the Minnesota Army National Guard. A while after completing bootcamp and additional training, marrying, and starting a family, I returned to school at Liberty University where I completed a bachelor's degree in social science with a concentration in religion.

By the time I completed my bachelor's degree, I had been employed as a youth counselor, child protection case aide, fathers' program coordinator, correctional worker, and responded to a sense of call to ministry. A year or so after completing my bachelor's degree, I enrolled in Bethel Seminary where I completed twenty-four hours towards a Master of Divinity but did not complete the program. Several years later, I returned to school at Concordia University Saint Paul and completed a master's degree in family life education.

With the definition of social work in mind, it is probably clear by now that my preparation and entry to the profession of social work was not a linear process. My journey started with my first exposure to social work in a professional context while working as an on-call and full-time youth counselor at a detention center with youth that had been involved in inappropriate sexual behavior. Social workers would stop by and visit these young men and coordinate visits between them and their families. The social workers also facilitated the young men's transition back into their communities as well. I then transitioned to a full-time position as a case aide with Olmsted County child protection. It is in this role that I became aware of the fact that social work is more than simply "doing good" or "helping". I learned that it is about genuinely connecting with the hearts and minds of people experiencing various kinds of difficulties for different reasons to find what is often "the least messy" solution to life's challenges. In addition, it is connecting while endeavoring to manage important and appropriate boundaries because social work engages every aspect of a worker: personal and cultural experiences, past trauma, beliefs, values, and world views.

Following my role of case aide, I had opportunities to serve in the capacities of a Dads' Program coordinator/case manager, Project HOPE case manager, child protection social worker, child protection supervisor and program manager. Each opportunity created spaces for me to reflect on the intersection between my personal and professional development in the field of social work. I am grateful that all but one of these opportunities came while I was employed by Olmsted County in

Rochester, MN. During my employment at Olmsted County in Child and Family Services, I experienced a culture that prioritized collaboration, learning, professional development, quality individual and group supervision, innovation, and cultural humility. Along with a host of committed and talented supervisors, I was fortunate to be exposed to social work experts and models like Dr. Sue Lohrbach, Ann Ahlquist, Dr. Andrew Turnell, Larry Hopwood, and Nikki Weld. I was also furnished with books written by pioneer clinicians, Insoo Kim Berg and Steve de Shazer.

The quality of supervision and professional training greatly shaped my thinking and approach as a practitioner and human services leader. I am convinced that the organizational culture of Olmsted County Child and Family Services was ideal for developing a person of my background and experiences because it promoted learning, reflection, and application which stimulated my personal and professional growth. I am grateful for all that I received during my employment with Olmsted County. I continue to bring forward these experiences in my present role as Senior Administrative Manager with Hennepin County Human Services where I manage the work of an equity navigator, three community engagement coordinators, a Safe and Connected Coordinator, and oversee staffing management, and payroll.

As I reflect on my journey into the profession of social work and human services more broadly, I have some advice for anyone considering social work as a profession. First, resist the temptation to think about the profession solely from the perspective of economics. While it isn't the highest paying field, it is a growing field that provides many avenues and settings for practice affording opportunities to achieve a livable wage. Second, reflect upon your experiences within your own family of origin and other lived experiences. There are studies that suggest a relationship between social work students' history of psychosocial trauma or experience early in life and their selection of social work as a chosen profession (Esaki & Larkin, 2013). Trauma in life doesn't have to be a barrier to a successful career in social work if engaged intentionally and constructively. Every social worker brings their experiences, values, beliefs, and culture to their work. Third, when selecting an employer, do your homework and, where possible, seek out organizations that have a "restorative culture" (Esaki and Larkin 35). Organizations that have reflective cultures prioritize reflective supervision and practice, ongoing professional development, attunement to the importance of the parallel process, and overt efforts to communicate a deep respect for the lived experiences of individuals, families, and all communities in administration and service delivery.

Pearl of Wisdom

"Wherever your social work journey takes you, always remember, social work is about genuinely connecting with the hearts and minds of people experiencing various kinds of difficulties for different reasons to find what is often "the least messy" solution to life's challenges."
~ Gilbert Domally

ABOUT THE AUTHOR

Gilbert Domally began his career in human services as an on-call youth counselor in 1999. Since then, he has served in a variety of direct practice and leadership capacities. His experiences include youth counseling, program coordination, case management, child protection supervision and program management.

Gil holds a Bachelor of Science with concentrations in social science and religion from Liberty University and Master of Arts in Family Life Education from Concordia University Saint Paul. Gil was certified as a family life educator in 2013 and became a licensed graduate social worker in 2015.

He is currently employed by Hennepin County as a Senior Administrative Manager in Human Services overseeing equity work, community engagement, staffing management and payroll, and implementation of the Safe and Connected Consultation and Information Sharing Framework.

Gil is a husband and father of six children and three grandchildren. He currently resides in the Minneapolis Metro.

LinkedIn: linkedin.com/in/gil-domally-ma-a5896a31

7

COURTNEY AABERG, LBSW

PERSEVERING ON PURPOSE

WHY SOCIAL WORK? It seems odd that I can't pinpoint the moment I reached such a monumental decision in my life. I am curious if this happens to all adolescents who don't excel in math or science; an automatic bid to a career in social sciences. *Just kidding.* In all seriousness, my teenage years proved to be a formative time of shaping my values and career aspirations, especially in regards to mental health. I had little understanding of the subject at the time because it wasn't freely discussed or recognized as anything other than "bad behavior." I observed mental health struggles in my peers with little accessibility in our own community and school to physicians, counselors, or social workers to offer individualized strategies. I was naturally drawn to being a listening ear for others and learning more about their unique circumstances. It felt meaningful to devote my time to being a support to others navigating life's difficulties even when I wasn't necessarily qualified to do so.

I hail from Rothsay, Minnesota, a rural, farming community with less than five hundred residents (mostly of Scandinavian descent), a K-12 school, and prairie chickens running amok. You read that correctly: prairie chickens. It may be worth your time to pause here and browse Google images in amazement. This tight-knit, wonderful community has been home to my dad's family for generations. Like most small towns, the mantra "it takes a village" rings true as you know most everyone and they certainly know you. You can't get away with much in this type of environment, for better or for worse. My background is noteworthy because, without this familial, community of support I grew up with, the trajectory of my life could have been very different.

I would soon rely on this community of support when, in the summer before I entered fifth grade, my life drastically changed. Shortly after returning home from vacation to Yellowstone National Park with our family of five, my mom died. Her journey with breast cancer was now complete after a courageous effort to rid her body of the relentless disease. Cancer was no match for her undeniable strength and beauty. Even so, her life ended and the world kept spinning. But for me, it didn't. Everything was different and nothing would ever be the same. *I would never be the same.* It was impossible to comprehend such a significant loss with only ten years of living under my belt. And so began my first experience of living with a broken heart.

Without hesitation, our community rallied around my dad, older sister, my younger brother, and myself in ways that won't be forgotten. My memories of acute grief during this time are limited. However, I do know there was endless hotdish (Minnesotan for casserole), countless sleepovers with friends, and oddly, stability. In the face of unimaginable change to our family unit, my dad, with the help of extended family and friends, kept our lives as stress-free as possible. Later I would come to understand this was a privilege in itself. Life continued on, much differently than before, and people stepped up to mend the newly formed cracks in our hearts. Without teachers, coaches, my friends' parents, and countless others taking stock of my life and cultivating meaningful relationships with me, it could have been easy to rely on unhealthy avenues for coping with grief. I know not everyone is afforded these same supports in life and it became largely important to me to pay it forward.

In college, I studied Human Development and Family Science and Social Work through a dual-degree program at North Dakota State University in conjunction with Minot State University. This field of study piqued my interest immediately as it felt like an appropriate direction given my interest in human behavior, relationships, and channeling empathy into a career path. One of the greatest strengths of the social work profession, in my opinion, is the continuous opportunity for introspection. Topics of study often labeled as "uncomfortable

66

subjects" and not encouraged at a dinner party were par for the course in class. Constantly challenging the beliefs and biases you grew up with for further examination proved to be essential to broaden my limited perspective of the world. Specifically, I remember reading *Unpacking the Invisible Knapsack* and feeling great shame for the privilege I was afforded due to my skin color; I never fully comprehended the unjust, oppressive systems our society continues to perpetuate on people of color to this day. It was a very important topic for me to face head on, especially after growing up in a community with very little diversity. My perspective of the world only grew richer through the stories I read or learned from others with different experiences. This type of critical thinking is special to the social work field, and for that I'm grateful.

Social work also provides a concise foundation for practice through a code of ethics and core values: ***service, social justice, dignity and worth of the person, importance of human relationships, integrity, and competence***. This set of principles is essential for fine-tuning the necessary skills of being a competent social worker. For someone who thrives on rules and structure, it was a great guideline for the expectations of working in a helping profession. Even with a set code and established values, each professional must consider personal strengths and weaknesses. One of the most challenging parts of this field for me continues to be setting firm boundaries with clients. How can I provide resources and problem-solving strategies to support independence without becoming personally invested in the way I'd solve a crisis? Am I enabling versus empowering? Many of these core values and important lessons can be taught but never understood until you enter the workforce and put them into practice.

My internship at Lakeland Mental Health Center (LMHC) in Moorhead, Minnesota gave me the ability to work directly with children and their families while coordinating mental health services. One of the greatest assets of the agency is the number of services offered in-house including: psychiatry, psychotherapy, case management, adult rehabilitative (ARMHS), children's therapeutic services and supports (CTSS), day treatment, and crisis services. The accessibility to other providers offers a great advantage for care coordination on all levels. I saw firsthand how an individual's mental health trickles into every aspect of their life, and how beneficial supports within the community, school, and home are for stabilization of symptoms. I observed just how difficult it can be for families to surrender themselves to the idea that they cannot manage everything on their own. My past experiences never allowed me to forget that *it takes a village*. Why is there the expectation that they should do it all alone? I'm often inspired by clients and their families for allowing providers into their circle of trust, so to speak. It's not always that simple, but opening their everyday routines and habits up for debate to total strangers is no easy feat. The amount of growth I encountered—sometimes small, but nonetheless growth—left me invigorated for the future.

When it came time to graduate into adulthood, it was an easy choice. Why wouldn't I stay with an agency that allowed me the privilege (let's be honest…oftentimes, the challenge) to walk alongside clients and support their needs for a better quality of life? Isn't that what we are all after? To be better than we were yesterday? When I first began full-time, I worked with clients in the adult service department to provide adult rehabilitative mental health services (ARMHS). This position allowed me to work with individuals to strengthen their independent living skills and social competencies affected by their mental health diagnoses. A few months later, I found myself accepting the position of Rule 79 case manager in children's services, right where my internship had begun, and I haven't looked back since. I'd hate to lead you on and paint a picture that my entire social work career has been sunshine and rainbows, because that isn't accurate. There has been frustration, burnout, and the overwhelming feeling that my attempts to support others have little impact. Oftentimes, this means adjusting my expectations and re-evaluating my role in specific situations. Despite the tough times, working with kids continues to be an area of passion for me, and I'm lucky to be surrounded by others who feel the same.

I would be remiss if I didn't devote a little time to boast about the community of social workers and mental health practitioners I've come to consider as family. I am surrounded by incredibly compassionate, hard-working individuals whose goals align with my own. Each one brings their own unique set of experiences to the table which often makes for spirited case consultations. There is nothing quite like Department 31. The family dynamic that has been created is invaluable, especially in a high burnout career. There is a reason I haven't "left the nest" even when different opportunities have become available. Working with individuals that genuinely care for my well-being makes all the difference, and I'm fully aware of how rare that type of work environment can be. Not only can our social workers be counted on to show up for their clients, but they'll show up for their friends too.

September 8, 2020 is another date filled with drastic, life-changing events for me. Roughly six months into a global pandemic, everyone was still trying to make sense of the new protocols and changes happening on a daily basis. Yet somehow, by the end of this day, the pandemic seemed like small potatoes. Jordan, my husband of three years and partner for the last eleven years, would die unexpectedly in our home while we watched TV. This traumatic event left me shattered and unsure how to proceed in life with our sweet one-year-old daughter, Delia, to raise on my own. How could the motherless daughter raise the now fatherless daughter? I'm not equipped for this. Luckily, no one asked me to be. There was an immediate influx of visitors to my home, more hotdish, and an outpouring of love and support. It felt all too familiar. Through the haze of the first few days after my husband's death, I can't remember many of the conversations I had, but I do recall who showed up. My people. Past and present members of Department 31 were at my home completing a landscaping project that was left unfinished. This act of kindness didn't surprise me in the least and it was one of the moments I felt most at peace in the early days of my grief.

Grief. Cue the first line of Simon and Garfunkel's "Sound of Silence": "*Hello darkness my old friend.*" Grief was my trusty companion and more prominent than ever. I had learned from my mother's death that it was not something that could be set aside or ignored. Something I had learned to carry with me now grew to suffocate me with its larger-than-life re-emergence to the forefront of my life. There is no amount of preparation or pessimism about life that prepares you for circumstances out of your control. Grief doesn't look the same person to person, but it changes them from the inside out. You can't outrun it. *I've tried.* I was already painfully aware of these truths after losing my mom at a young age. I knew that this time I could not count on myself to get through it without help. Thankfully, this time I was better equipped to seek out help in order to navigate this new phase of my life.

Enter grief counseling. This marked my first experience venturing to a professional for help and undoubtedly not my last. It takes an incredibly special person to support others in their vulnerability. She too was a social worker. Somehow, this made what I knew would be an uncomfortable starting point on my grief journey a little easier. Beginning to work through my grief became a very important puzzle piece of the healing process. I was met with compassion, reflective listening, education, and other invaluable tools to help me take life one day at a time, and sometimes the timeline was smaller. During a session with my grief counselor, I once described losing my husband as having all of the air sucked out of the room. In the early days of my traumatic grief, I was completely paralyzed by any decision, little or big. It often felt like I was being suffocated by an invisible force. Some days, this still proves true. Thankfully, I didn't let even the worst days stop me from "doing the work." That's not to say some days of living in denial aren't essential for my survival too. The more the grief fog clears in my mind, the more I'm left wondering how to make sure my experience was not in vain. What could come of this personal tragedy that could bring goodness into the world?

So, naturally, I put on my case manager hat and began to brainstorm. Questions flooded my mind. How are newly widowed parents managing funeral planning, household responsibilities, and finances on top of day-to-day schedules? These are essentials that must be done, and doesn't even account for time for grief itself. Personally, I took an entire month off from my job to keep my life afloat. This would not have been possible without support from my employer, PTO donations, life insurance, GoFundMe fundraising, and support from family and friends. Every day was spent checking off tasks on my to-do list including making painstaking phone calls to service providers asking to take my husband's name off our account and ensuring I wouldn't miss any payments. All of these responsibilities were exhausting and filled me with endless wonder about what other widows or widowers do without employment or the other forms of support I had in times like this. How is it that even in grief, the most human experience you can have, there are so many disparities? I would love for greater accessibility of grief resources in every community, and for expansion of services beyond counseling or support groups to accommodate the challenges that accompany the disruptive nature of death. It's clear that there is always more we can do.

Now that I've surely brightened your day with everyone's favorite topics of death and grief, I'd like to introduce a little hope. Life has not always been easy, and I'm completely prepared for the fact that it could get more difficult with or without my consent. Even so, on the hardest days,

I try to find beauty in things happening right now. One of the things that I cling to on my saddest days continues to be my role as a social worker. Helping others continues to help me learn and grow into a better person. It puts into perspective what's most important at the end of the day. For me, that's people. What is life without the people we pass our time with?

So…what next? *Where will social work lead me?* As my experiences in life continue to shape my interests, especially in the grief realm, I hope to someday find myself lending a hand to others navigating the overwhelming challenges that come with losing a loved one. Whether that looks like connecting others to resources, advocating for policy change with bereavement leave, or educating others about the complexities of grief, I know one thing for sure: the possibilities are endless. The social work field has an abundance of avenues to pursue as my passions evolve. That's why at the end of the day, I'd be surprised to find myself too far from it. I better go engage in some self-care before I re-think my last statement. While it's not a profession for the faint of heart, the opportunity to walk alongside others often in a vulnerable capacity is one that I continue to hold close to my heart.

Pearl of Wisdom
"Open your mind to the possibility that life will look nothing like you imagined. Go forth with bold perseverance anyway. You're gonna need it."
~ Courtney Aaberg

ABOUT THE AUTHOR

Courtney Aaberg, LSW is a Rule 79 Children's Mental Health Targeted Case Manager/Children's Therapeutic Services and Supports practitioner at Lakeland Mental Health Center in Minnesota. In this role, Courtney coordinates mental health services that provide direct rehabilitative intervention to children living with severe emotional disturbance diagnoses. Courtney is recently widowed, aspiring to find strength in the struggle of life's most unpredictable seasons. She resides in North Dakota with her daughter.

LinkedIn: https://www.linkedin.com/in/courtney-aaberg-7b6156b8

8

JESS HOEPER, MSW, LISW

THE POWER OF A CONNECTED MOMENT

I WAS SITTING outside my high school counselor's office, full of excitement and anticipation. It was, after all, senior student career planning day. *What should I do with the rest of my life?* I had wondered this so many times throughout this senior year and today was the day to make a plan! As I waited outside the counselor's office I thought about my top choices: Boston, NYC or abroad. I needed to leave, of that I was certain. I had started to notice some unhealthy relationships I was participating in—although I did not yet have full awareness, I was participating in the unhealthy relationships due to unresolved trauma. I patted myself on the back for making a bold decision to be fully present and future-focused for this career planning session. I had taken the career placement tests and many helping professions showed up in the results across social work, teaching, counseling, etc. These all sounded appropriate; I care about people and feel strongly that everyone is worthy of love and belonging. A helping career would fit me well. So back to where we were, I was sitting outside my counselor's office. While waiting I had grounded myself in some bold decisions. I would be a teacher and go to Boston to fulfill that path. I didn't even know what schools were in Boston. I decided that would be the focus of my counseling time, we will figure out which school I will attend in Boston for a teaching degree.

It was my turn, she welcomed me into her office and quickly started the conversation: "So, what alternatives to college have you thought about?" .... wait, what?!?! "What do you mean?" I asked. She proceeded, "Well your grade point average is low, so you are unlikely to get into a traditional college, and certainly no out-of-state options will be accessible." This moment altered what I thought possible for myself. This moment was one of those pivotal moments that demonstrated the power that is held in a single moment when you are in a helping profession. I was rocked by this disconnected moment, but I am also forever grateful for the profound experiential learning it provided. This realization of the power within a single moment would shape my helping career.

It took me a bit of time to put all the pieces together about how powerful this moment was and how deeply connected to other creative wounds it could become. Yet, when I reflected on this moment in my counselor's office, I began to realize how profoundly aware of pivotal moments I was and had always been. I was now celebrating the awareness that I had often been able to find meaning in what others could see as meaningless moments. I found a strength in reflection that I was unaware had existed so strongly in myself for as far back as I could remember. I thought back to other trajectory/path building moments in my early life that shaped who I was in that young adult moment. I had some deep creative wounds that had stuck with me, but not in tragic ways, more in a deep understanding of the unintentional consequences that come when helpers connect with others in an unaware frame of mind. My counselor wasn't consciously there to ruin my day or alter my life path in a negative way, but she did have that power within that moment to alter my experience. This is when I found my ability to see rejection as simply redirection.

This is where I start my journey to social work, for the purpose of this journey story. This is by no means holistic of my life journey story, which does of course play a part in my path to and into social work. Let me lay a bit of my developmental foundation. I was gifted and given safety in childhood from birth to eighteen years old. I had available and caring parents, who provided trust, safety, and an understanding that I was worthy as a person. I grew up in a safe community, my personal safety was never a direct worry. Every adversity, I had support. Every traumatic event, I had support. Every impulsive mistake, I had support. Every heartbreak, I had support. It is from this support that I was given the gift of ability to be curious! Curious I was and curious I still am! In fact, I have now built a career that uses curiosity and wonder in action, through Reflective Coaching with human service professionals and leaders. However, I did not go from the hallway of my school counselor's office to reflective coaching!

I was seventeen when I graduated high school and started college as an adult new to adulthood. It would be very early in my college career that I would come face to face with unresolved trauma. Because of the developmental safety my parents had created in adolescence, things that had been *traumatic* had not become *trauma*. The traumatic experience had little impact on my functioning as an adolescent but *would* later have an impact on my young adult functioning. I did not trust my body or my mind as a woman. My trauma was tricking my instincts. I had fears that I was not aware were so strong, the fears were irrational and rooted in PTSD. One of the clearest moments of connection to self was, when I was on a walk on a very safe street in broad daylight. I felt complete terror, an irrational terror, that someone would jump out of the bushes and attack me. But at this very moment, I heard the *Divine* voice within my intuition tell me in the clearest of sounds, "Trauma can trick your instincts, but it can never touch your intuition." That connected moment would imprint the strength of **connection to self**.

I wouldn't know of social work as a profession for several years. After the school counselor meeting, I would decide to attend the local university where my mom worked. I first chose teaching, then chose criminal justice, then tried speech pathology, until finally I just wanted to get done with college and start working with people and landed in sociology. Those were the courses that I was strongest in and I graduated with a Sociology Degree.

During my junior year of college, I solicited the intervention of the Divine in my intimate relationships. On a piece of paper, I put all the qualities I desired and needed in a partner: loving, fiercely loyal, funny, strong sense of self, etc. Then I put that paper away in a safe place, and left the rest up to the Divine. I met Alan six months later, and he had all the qualities I asked for. We got married!

After graduation, I started working in the field of mental health and came into direct contact with social workers. I wondered, "Who are these people and what is this role?" I learned quickly that my values and personality were a good fit for this new field of social work. I went back to school to finish the courses needed for a social work degree, but my undergraduate degree in social work would only come after rejections from two graduate schools in fields *around* social work.

When I finished my social work degree, Alan and I were expecting our first child and moving across the state to a brand-new location for my husband's career. I was finally leaving, although the strong desire to fly that I had as an adolescent was gone. Now, moving/leaving felt necessary but very different. We didn't move too far from family. I am the oldest of two and my brother was still within the same state, and my parents only a couple of hours away. My husband and I value being connected to our family; he is after all the baby of ten children and his relationship with his mother is very strong. I would learn just how strong and how much I valued the strength of their relationship, when later in this journey, actually our now as I pen this chapter, we decided to move next door to his mother! We moved across the state to start our family life together. I started my social work professional career as a juvenile justice social worker; an undergraduate stint in criminal justice and a degree in social work married well in this space. A series of career events propelled me into child welfare: the juvenile justice position would be cut, and I would find myself in the most dysfunctional workplace I have ever been in. As a result of this dysfunction, I would see the posting for a high-risk child protection social work position, apply, and start in the field of child welfare. I haven't looked back since! This is also when I decided to attend graduate school for social work. Completing my Master's in Social Work (MSW) is one of my proudest career accomplishments.

Back to my journey into child welfare. I would not have chosen the field of child welfare, for many of the same reasons others say they wouldn't choose it. However, the families and kids you meet and have the honor of working with change you in a way no one can prepare you for! My curiosity of "problems" was ignited at a soul level. I would see life experiences labeled as "problems" and wonder, "Who decides what a problem is?" and "How do they decide?" This led me back in reflection to my educational experience in high school. I was a student that got a D in an English class, not because I *couldn't* do the work, but because I *didn't* do the work. So, was the D the problem? Nope! For me, it was the lack of connection to why the work was important. The grade would later become important, as you saw in the opening of this journey, but should that have been the focus? This is how I approach family system "problems". It is very infrequent that families or children don't care; it is that they aren't connected to the need for a solution. They lack hope.

My business is built around the idea of *active hope*. Hope to me is made active by **H**elping **O**ther **P**eople **E**veryday. This message of how to activate hope was gifted to me at my grandfather's funeral. This is the most poignant moment of a **connection to the collective** I have had to date! At my grandfather's funeral, I was wearing a bracelet that spelled out HOPE: four cubes, each with a letter. My grandfather was the most giving, involved, connected man I knew. He helped whoever needed help. At the funeral, I was spinning the cubes on this bracelet. As the pastor was talking about how "Ray helped other people every-day," I was spinning each cube with my fingertips. In that moment, time slowed down. I heard that deeply familiar Divine voice putting the pieces together. "*H* is Help, *O* is Other, *P* is People and *E* is Everyday. Hope is made active by helping other people everyday." My life's mission was set and etched onto my heart. This would fuel my social work mission then and to this day.

To activate hope for families and children, I knew I needed to build strong relationships and be connected to them. I can remember the power of a connected moment in child welfare like it was yesterday. I was with a mother of three teenagers. She came into the child protection system due to a report of physical abuse. The identified problem was that she had physically hurt her kids. But the problem to be reme-died by child welfare would not actually *be* the hitting of her kids. The hitting would stop once she was seen and had alternatives to fix her identified "problem". One afternoon, she let me in as she had done several times before, but today she would be screaming mad, pounding on the stove mad, standing within proximity that I could feel her breath mad, but I had no sense of worry. I felt calm in her crisis, because I saw her. We *were connected.* I saw a terrified mom with a well-honed skill of anger activating her to be physical. I also saw a mom with an urgent desire to keep her adolescents safe from harm, who felt as though she had no alternatives to hitting. Intergenerational transmission of trauma came across clearly. She was doing what had been done to her. She had not considered an alternative because no one spent the time to walk through this hard space with her. The power of **connection to others** was clear.

I had a strong awareness of the power of helping in relationships with children and families; being genuinely connected to them no matter the circumstances that brought us to know each other. But it would not be until an unassuming woman from New Zealand named Nicki Weld would come to provide a training on *professional dangerousness* that I would realize the intense need for curiosity of self in the work—the type of curiosity that builds self-awareness within the work. I saw how my unawareness could actually be contributing to the harm a family is experiencing. Child welfare scholar, Tony Morrison, and his colleagues originally defined professional dangerousness as "the processes whereby professionals behave in ways that collude with or increase the dangerous dynamics of a family" (Morrison, 1990). I have made it part of my current work's mission to enhance the understanding around this topic that almost quite literally knocked me off my chair. This topic changed my understanding of self and in turn drastically changed my practice. I was forced to reckon with my own biases, beliefs, and values which otherwise could become the burden of the children and/or families. The clearest example of this is my engagement with a father I had worked with. This dad was hard to connect with. Usually, I did not by nature shy away from engaging families, in fact engagement was one my strengths. However, when this dad challenged me, I was unaware of how to navigate the relationship and that made it his burden to bear. I struggled to engage him and would put him at the bottom of my to-do list. In hindsight, this was unfair for this father who as we know in social work, likely had an anchor of pain to why he was hard to engage with. It wasn't his burden to bear as the recipient, but mine as the professional! When I started seeing these things in myself, I couldn't help but start to feel very passionate about letting everyone in the field know and really letting the world know about this topic!

Following this profound learning about professional dangerousness and my graduate research on compassion fatigue, I decided to move into supervision. I came face to face with professional dangerousness from a different vantage point: viewing the system failure in a way I had not previously been privy to. I found very well-intended and brilliant workers bogged down by system process constraints that left them with an inability to deeply connect with children and families, which led to very high levels of professional dangerousness. I learned that professional dangerousness is not just behaviors acted out by professionals, but also by communities, collaborative partners, and organizations. Professional dangerousness is an *entire* system issue, not just a worker issue.

I decided to leave my supervision position, and my husband and I moved our family to his family farm. After settling into the farm, we turned our family of six into our completed family of seven. It was here that I would get to intentionally consider what I really wanted to do within the social work field and life. I began teaching as an adjunct professor and developed a child welfare topics course. I found a love for writing, both professional and just for fun. Writing for fun led me to my first published piece. I co-authored a book titled *Success Codes* with other inspiring women from around the world. I even had space to say yes to research projects.

My current role as business owner and reflective coach has afforded me the opportunity to work *with* the child welfare and public human service systems without the need to work directly *within*. I believe that you cannot teach or participate in a class from the hallway. To change what you see needs changing, you have to actively participate in the change making. My current work allows me space to be innovative and develop ways to support those doing the work, anchored in the belief that parallel process is strong. If those that are doing the work are thriving, the work done will be thriving. If the work done is thriving, then the recipients are more likely to be thriving. It is my role to build and enhance awareness for those doing the work, and I hope it activates others to find space where they can have their greatest impact. I remember this powerful adage: "Systems don't change. People change. And then people change the system." I am still navigating the world of social work and trying to find my way to be a participant in the change.

What I have learned from my journey to and within social work is, at its simplest, that there is true power in a connected moment. ***There is power in the connection to self, connection to others and connection to the collective.*** That connection is built through moments of presence. Awareness of the power of connection is built within reflection. I feel charged, challenged, and grateful to be within the social work profession at this moment of time and history. There is work to do, and all the work should be anchored in love.

Pearl of Wisdom

"You can never fully know the power within a moment of connection until the moment is reviewed through reflection, but you can be certain that every connected moment is enhanced if you are fully present."

~ Jess Hoeper

ABOUT THE AUTHOR

Jessica Hoeper, MSW|LISW|IMH-E® Infant Family Specialist has been in the field of social work for over 15 years. Jess is the owner of Ray of HOPE, LLC. Ray of Hope offers Reflective Coaching to Human Service Leaders/Professionals and Child Welfare enhancement trainings nationally. Jess's reflective coaching offers leaders a space to enhance their self awareness, feel through the uncomfortable, and increase their vigor for building a system that prioritizes relationships! Jess is an adjunct social work instructor at St. Scholastica. Jess also enjoys speaking and writing. Jess participates in local column writing and is a co-author of an award-winning/internationally best-selling book "Success Codes: Secrets to success you weren't taught in school." Jessica and her husband Alan live on a farm in central Minnesota with their five children, Hannah, Henry, Harris, Hayes and Hogan.

Website: www.rayofhopereflectivecoaching.com
Instagram: @reflective_coaching
LinkedIn: Jessica Hoeper
YouTube: Ray of Hope Reflective Coaching

9

YACENIA MURLEE Q. CRISOSTOMO, MSW, LSWAIC, MHP

TRAVELING LIGHT

WHEN I FIRST BEGAN THE journey to become a social worker, I did not know how to answer the question often posed to me: "Why would you choose such a hard career?" I used to tell people that I did not choose social work; social work chose me. Now, that is not to say that was not the truth because, at one point, I did not dream of being a social worker. I had dreams of becoming a singer, then a desire to be a journalist, and even contemplated a career in the medical field. But as an adult, I have come to understand that I continued to pursue the social work profession with the hope that I would eventually become what I needed since I was a child. I wanted to become what had inspired me to speak up and not give up: a social worker.

As a child, I was always told, "What happens at home, stays at home." So, whenever someone of authority asked me, "What is wrong?" or, "What happened?" I already had my lines rehearsed. I did not share the memories I had of my father strangling my mother while he was drunk during elementary school. I did not tell anyone how many times I had to beg for my sister not to take her own life while I attended middle school. I even denied it whenever someone challenged whether the sex with a nineteen-year-old was consensual or not, even when I knew that I did not want it to happen at thirteen years old. I lied about how many drinks I had every night after leaving an abusive husband at twenty years old, and I denied the times I contemplated driving off a bridge to escape the pain of losing everything. I always feared what would happen if I were honest about what was "happening at home." The truth behind what was happening to me remained hidden until I met a social worker; one of my professors while I attended Saint Martin's University.

I had many conversations with other professionals, but the first conversation I had with this professor was different. At the time, everything was going wrong with me. I had recently re-enrolled back into undergraduate classes at Saint Martin's University, left an abusive marriage, and was attempting to find a purpose in life again. My grades were falling apart, I felt hopeless, and I was ready to give up, and this professor could see it. I am not sure what it was about her office, but in speaking with my other classmates, I learned that this professor's office was where people walked in and, within five minutes, were crying and pouring their souls out to her. This professor was not mean, and she did not judge me for my mistakes in her class or in any other parts of my life. This professor listened, she held space for my emotions, and for once in my life, I felt like I could trust someone with what was really "happening at home." By the end of this first conversation, I had learned that there are people in the world that will listen, hold space, and not judge you for your actions. At the end of this conversation, I had decided that I wanted to be that kind of person: a social worker.

For two years following that conversation, life continued to dig a deeper "rock bottom." I struggled to maintain decent grades, worked multiple jobs to survive, and spent more time taking naps in my car than I did sleeping in an actual bed. I had re-enrolled in full-time classes at Saint Martin's University and was on my way to achieving a bachelor's degree, no matter what it took. By this time, flashbacks of my childhood trauma became more persistent and my ability to hide memories and pain lessened. Even throughout these challenges, my professor continued to guide me and hold space for me while I fought to make it to the finish line. At times, I doubted whether I could continue forward and even pleaded for someone to let me give up and give in. But this professor continued to hold hope where I once felt hopeless. I spent my last year in my undergraduate program working seventy hours a week and studying in and out of class for an additional twenty hours a week with little time to sleep or eat. Fortunately, I crossed this race's finish line in May 2016 when I received my Bachelor's degree in Social Work. The next race began shortly after I decided to obtain my

Master's in Social Work from Simmons University (formerly Simmons College).

During graduate school, I continued to develop this ability to "sit with" and hold space for others to process their emotions, as it had once been done for me. Unfortunately, I had not yet learned how to do that for myself, so concern for countertransference quickly appeared while I was working to complete my last internship as a therapist in Yuma, Arizona. It was through this internship that I was confronted with the ugly truth that I could not continue to excel as a social worker without first showing up for myself and doing my own work. Thus, I began participating in eye-movement desensitization and reprocessing (EMDR) therapy to address the mountain of trauma that I had been carrying around with me since I was a child. With the assistance of yet another social worker, I began to see that it was possible to come from a broken home, a troubled past, and still choose to do the work to be different and do better. In fact, I did better and achieved greater than I could have ever imagined. I received my Master's in Social Work in May 2020, and beyond that, I finally found a voice to speak the truth.

Now when I speak to others, whether it is as a social worker in a clinical setting or to a friend in my personal life, I speak without fear of my inner child saying the wrong thing. I speak to the inner child of all individuals who have spent years trying to cover up their pain out of fear. I speak to those who, like me, were not allowed to speak of what happened behind closed doors and are in need of someone to hold space. I speak to those who hate answering questions about their upbringing and about their home life because of the feeling that it never goes anywhere; it never brings help or hope. I speak to those who seem to have it all together from the outside, but on the inside are looking for something to call their own light in a dark tunnel. For me, my dark tunnel was my childhood, my truth, and all the things that were "happening at home" throughout all these years. But now, I can say that social work is the light I needed to find a way through that tunnel. Social work became my purpose for navigating all the grief, trauma, and pain in my life. Most especially, becoming a social worker meant that I would need to confront my childhood demons and all my wounds. The same wounds I once swore I would never speak of became the same wounds that would ultimately set me free. The same wounds that I feared being exposed are the same wounds that are slowly healing with time, patience, and self-love. Now, I practice carrying less. I stopped practicing how to hold still and wait for the storm to pass. Instead, I am learning how to travel even when things are scary, hard, and painful. It is now my hope that all who choose to take a similar journey will offload what they cannot carry any longer and pick up all things love, light, and joy.

Pearl of Wisdom
"Travel Light. Unpack Often."
~ Yacenia Murlee Q. Crisostomo

ABOUT THE AUTHOR

Yacenia Crisostomo is a Licensed Independent Clinical Social Work Associate and Mental Health Professional. She currently provides individualized therapeutic intervention and case management services for those living with delusional and/or mood disorders in multiple psychiatric settings. Her professional life includes mental health counseling for children, families, and individuals who have experienced trauma and loss. Driven by her own healing journey, Yacenia is committed to working with survivors of abuse. She does this by offering support and guidance while they work through negative beliefs and develop self-love. Yacenia continues to share her story of trauma, grief, and resiliency with hope that it will be a light for those trying to find a way through their own dark tunnels.

Instagram: https://www.instagram.com/yazcxo/
Email: crisostomoymq@gmail.com

Photo Credit: Cheyenne Monteiro Photography, LLC

HILARY N. WEAVER, DSW

A SOCIAL WORK JOURNEY: WINNING
VICTORIES FOR HUMANITY

THE BREADTH of what social workers do and our keystone values of service and social justice have made this profession a comfortable fit for many types of people, myself included. I remember telling a school guidance counselor I wanted to be a social worker long before I understood the profession. Social work has taken me to conferences and speaking engagements around the world. I have spoken at the United Nations multiple times and have done mitigation work for multiple prisoners on death row. In recent months, I was appointed the inaugural Global Indigenous Commissioner for the International Federation of Social Workers (IFSW) and became the first Indigenous Chair-elect of the Board of Directors of the Council on Social Work Education (CSWE). My primary roles encompass taking social work skills and values into different external spaces, and working as a change agent within, helping our profession live up to its potential. This chapter recounts highlights of that journey and illustrates the many places where social work has taken me.

I was born and raised in Pullman, Washington, a small college town, where my parents taught at Washington State University. At that time, Eastern Washington State was an almost exclusively White region with most of the limited ethnic diversity coming from international students attending the university. In elementary school, I remember three of us who were "showcased" annually for being "different": one Jewish girl, one girl whose mother was from Japan and father was a White American serviceman, and me. I had no sense of myself as a cultural being other than knowing I was considered different. In the second grade, one teacher told the class I had olive skin. I found this a bizarre and unsettling assertion, since I knew full well that olives were green, and I was definitely not green.

My mother was Lakota and my father was White Appalachian—what that side of my family would call hillbilly. As an only child thousands of miles away from any relatives, I grew up unconnected to family or heritage. Although the 1960s was a time of racial activism and cultural pride in many parts of the United States, Pullman remained a sheltered environment and my parents deliberately tried to raise me as a generic, color-blind person. Despite my parents' intentions, it was clear that others saw me as different and tried to categorize and make sense of me rather than simply allowing me to be human.

Two major childhood events influence how I think about difference and how I see myself today. When I was nine, my parents and I lived in Spain for two years, which at the time was ruled by Fascist dictator Generalissimo Francisco Franco. I remember my mother explaining that dictators could be benevolent. I also remember political instability and bombings as the country struggled to determine whether it would return to monarchy or continue under military rule after the aging Franco's death. Living in Spain, I was more different than I had ever been before. I was put in a Catholic school knowing nothing about Catholicism, especially how it manifested within Spanish culture. I was surrounded by bloody images of tormented sinners and watched people march through the streets on their knees dragging chains as part of an Easter "parade". I also found myself in a classroom where nobody spoke English. I did not speak Spanish and as a result I experienced ridicule from teachers. These experiences of being foreign, not understanding the language, culture, politics, or religion of those around me indelibly shaped my perspectives.

Later, when I was in high school in Washington State, I became aware of an influx of new students, something highly unusual in a town where I had known most of my classmates since elementary school or before. These new students were in my school, but we had no interaction with them. No one explained who they were or why they were there. I was vaguely aware of American military involvement in Southeast Asia, but my understanding was limited by my age and by what information was publicly shared in the 1960s and 1970s. The US evacuated some American allies and their families following military withdrawal from Vietnam; those my age were enrolled in schools. I now reflect on the policy implications of refugee resettlement and how things could be done differently, bridging differences rather than enforcing separation.

In hindsight, my upbringing and early life experiences were both an advantage and liability. My parents made deliberate choices about where and how I was raised to try to shelter me from the racism and violence that were the backbone of social upheaval in the 1960s. This, however, did not change my appearance. The limited racial and ethnic diversity of the region led people like myself to be perceived as a curiosity more than a threat.

Once I left Washington State for college, I was frequently confronted with questions of where I was from. Being labeled as "different" was something that I absorbed and internalized, knowing that I would never be part of an "us" and would always be a "them". I spent time with my grandparents in search of community, looking for others like me. I pursued the intertwined questions of who I was as a person and who I would be as a social worker. The answers led me to focus my career on cultural issues in human services. I came to believe that cultural identity could be central for many human beings, even those raised to be color-blind and ostensibly culture-free.

As I decided where to study, Antioch College appealed to me. It was a place where I would spend half the year in the classroom and half in co-operative education opportunities. This would allow me to work in different capacities in three to six month blocks. For my first co-op experience, I moved to North Carolina and taught independent living skills at a group home for adults with developmental disabilities. My second placement took me to San Francisco where I worked as a play therapist in a hospital pediatric ward.

Antioch opened my eyes to social justice and what social work could be within that framework. The college motto became my guidepost: "*Be ashamed to die until you have won some victory for humanity.*" Antioch has a long history of embracing social justice. It admitted African American students when slavery persisted in the US and was the first US college to allow women to pursue a major of their choosing rather than being relegated to studying fields like home economics.

Two Antioch professors had a particularly enduring influence: Jewel Graham and Al Denman. Jewel taught classes in law and social work (Wikipedia contributors, 2021). She opened my eyes to a wide variety of social work content, but perhaps most meaningful was her transparency and critical thinking as she grappled with moral and ethical challenges. Jewel was the national President of the YWCA during my time at Antioch. She shared her dilemma when their world conference was held in South Africa during Apartheid. As an American she could attend with some level of privilege, but as an African American she struggled with whether her attendance would support the status quo of apartheid segregation. Her ability to share her decision-making process thoughtfully and openly with students provided an invaluable lesson I carry with me to this day.

Al Denman was another professor and role model whose example shaped my life (YS News Staff, 2019). He taught classes in law, religion, and philosophy. I later learned he saw his role at Antioch as partnering with Jewel as a type of "bookend" to students' academic experiences. As a straight, White, Christian, male (who was both a lawyer and ordained minister) he came from a position of privilege but chose to play a supporting role for Jewel, a woman of color. Al's classes took students outside their comfort zones. He required all papers cite diverse authors since we could not be fully informed if we were only drawing knowledge from White men from privileged backgrounds. Because of Al, I spent time in mosques, temples, and synagogues learning about people different than myself. These experiences informed my educational philosophy and influenced my use of experiential learning in teaching social work.

At Antioch I learned about a world of unfolding possibilities far from my sheltered upbringing. I chose to get my master's degree from Columbia University in the heart of New York City. There I could learn from notable social work scholars and be exposed to a variety of social circumstances and challenges. This training provided me with a skillset to make a difference as Antioch demanded. Even as I transitioned from direct practice to academia early in my career, I continued to take on roles where I used my social work skills.

After teaching social work at University of Idaho from 1988-1993, I accepted a faculty position at the School of Social Work at University at Buffalo. I became a member of the predominantly Haudenosaunee urban Native community in Western New York. I became involved with the Newtown Longhouse at Cattaraugus Reservation and was adopted into the Seneca Beaver Clan while retaining my Lakota identity.

In academia I found myself doing a lot of writing and presentations in addition to teaching. In these ways I could help other social workers and social work students understand the importance of cultural issues in the helping processes, thus making them better equipped to serve diverse populations, particularly Indigenous people and refugees. I found my voice and others found me. Social work has taken me many places, but I will highlight four experiences.

Death Row Mitigation

In 2000, I received a call from an attorney in a Federal Public Defender's Office who had seen my writing. She asked me to participate in mitigation work for a Native American prisoner on death row. My job as the social historian was to review thousands of pages of documents and conduct interviews. My knowledge of Native American cultures, my background as a social worker, and my understanding of trauma went into the report for the judge and subsequent testimony as an expert witness. My assessment could help a judge see a human being (including all the complexities of childhood trauma, poverty, addictions, racism, and failed child protective systems) and not define a person and their fate solely by horrific crimes. I have since done several mitigation cases for Native American prisoners on death row. The work is difficult and stressful but being part of processes that literally involve life and death decisions is one of the most important roles I have ever taken on as a social worker.

IFSW and the United Nations

For years, the United Nations (UN) worked on a document that would eventually be ratified in 2007 as the United Nations Declaration on the

Rights of Indigenous Peoples (United Nations, 2007). IFSW, through their work at the UN, monitored draft documents and developed their own statement on the Rights of Indigenous Peoples, grounded in the values and perspectives of the social work profession. The IFSW members drew on my writing while working on their statement and sought me out for comment. I gave input for the 2005 IFSW statement published on Indigenous Peoples (*Indigenous Peoples*, 2005). This connection grew, and I was invited to join the IFSW delegation to the UN Permanent Forum on Indigenous Issues in 2005, the first of many times I would speak there. I am proud to have helped bring a social work perspective to this large-scale international event.

Changing Mascots

When school district leaders in Lancaster, NY wanted to become more informed about the impact of Native American mascots as part of a decision-making process about their teams' name and logo, I joined four other local Native people to meet with the Superintendent and School Board. This change process became highly contentious and received national publicity. I met with student leaders to answer their questions and help them understand connections between mascots, stereotyping, racism, and self-esteem. My social work skills and understanding of theories about planned change helped ground and guide this highly divisive process. A structured community meeting allowed attendees with conflicting perspectives to share their thoughts and listen to others in small groups facilitated by social workers. The use of social workers at the community meeting to facilitate and mediate an explosive situation affirmed the importance of what our profession can bring to move society beyond divisions. In 2015, the Lancaster R******* became the Lancaster Legends.

Challenging Employment Discrimination

In 2016, my writing drew the attention of attorneys from the US Department of Justice (DOJ) who were suing a state, challenging employment discrimination for hiring human service professionals to work on a reservation. The DOJ documented a systematic process of hiring non-Native people with little to no professional qualifications or experience with Indigenous cultures to work on a reservation over

Native Americans who were immersed in the clients' culture and often had stronger professional credentials than the people who were ultimately hired. The DOJ hired me as an expert witness to document the importance of cultural competence in helping processes, something my whole career had prepared me to affirm. I provided written statements and participated in examinations and cross-examinations by attorneys. Armed with my testimony, the DOJ prevailed, and Native American human service professionals received settlements for the discrimination they had experienced. As a social worker, I played a key role in challenging discrimination and changing how a state hires human service workers.

Social work has taken me to many unexpected places. Many people have found my writings which have created additional opportunities for me and generated an unforeseen broader ripple effect. Occasionally I catch a glimpse of this impact. For example, I was approached by a young woman at a conference in Hualien, Taiwan who introduced herself as a social worker from the Philippines, noting my work had been meaningful for her. As an Indigenous student, she found it difficult to find social work resources that were considered acceptable scholarly sources by academic institutions while reflecting Indigenous community perspectives. My work bridged the Indigenous and the academic.

Social workers are change agents. I have found that it is indeed possible to change parts of the world, from helping school districts let go of stereotypical mascots to changing state employment practices to helping a judge consider a holistic perspective of a human being on death row. Reflecting on my career, I see two major themes: helping my chosen profession be responsive and accountable to those it serves and creating opportunities for others.

Helping social work be responsive and accountable is done through a combination of educating the next generation of social workers, sharing my knowledge through presentations and publications, and taking on professional leadership roles. I have held leadership roles in Native organizations including as Board Chair for Native American Community Services, an agency providing human services for the off-reservation community in Western New York. For the past quarter century, I have served as President of the Indigenous and Tribal Social Work Educators Association (ITSWEA), an organization that provides a safe space for Indigenous social workers, students, and educators who often find themselves invisible within our profession. ITSWEA gatherings provide an affirming space for those of us who walk both within the world of social work education and Indigenous communities. ITSWEA has also taken steps to hold our profession accountable, developing a Statement of Accountability and Reconciliation for Harms Done to Indigenous and Tribal Peoples that was passed unanimously by the CSWE Board of Directors in 2021 (Weaver et al., 2021).

I also bring an Indigenous voice to non-Indigenous spaces within social work. Previously, I served in regional roles with NASW in Idaho as well as on the national NASW board. I also served as Vice Chair/Secretary of the CSWE board and now serve as Chair-elect of the Board of Directors, being the first Indigenous person in that capacity. I have also proudly taken up a leadership position as the inaugural IFSW Global Indigenous Commissioner, facilitating the work of regional representatives from around the world.

The second theme that has become increasingly prominent as I reach the closing stages of my career is to hold doors open for others. I mentor Indigenous social workers and allies in writing, speaking, community engagement, and academia. Many doors have opened for me, and I have been truly blessed in this profession. If I can use the power and opportunities that I have been given to hold the door open for others, it will be a life and career well spent.

My work has evolved into being both an ambassador and a change agent for the social work profession. I am proud to be a social worker and believe our profession has a lot to offer. Our profession also needs to change, grow, and live up to its core values like social justice. I have found personal affirmation through making a difference for others.

I appreciate the holistic and inclusive nature of our profession when it is at its best. Social work has the potential to change the world. I embrace the breadth of our field and its foundation in social justice. Antioch taught me the importance of winning victories for humanity and the social work profession has given me a roadmap to do so.

Our profession is broad; there is no need to be all things to all people. The breadth of our profession means that we can share the load. We don't all need to be clinicians, policymakers, or researchers, yet social workers fill all these roles. As individual social workers, we can each find our niche and make a difference in this world, knowing that our profession is greater than the sum of its parts. We have a responsibility to make a difference in the lives of others and in our shared world.

Pearl of Wisdom
"We can win victories for humanity."
~ Hilary N. Weaver

ABOUT THE AUTHOR

Hilary N. Weaver, DSW (Lakota) is a Professor and Associate Dean for Diversity, Equity and Inclusion, School of Social Work, University at Buffalo. She received her BS from Antioch College and MSW and DSW from Columbia University. Her focus is on cultural issues in helping processes with an emphasis on Indigenous Peoples. Dr. Weaver is Chair-elect of the CSWE board of directors, Global Indigenous Commissioner for IFSW, and President of the Indigenous and Tribal Social Work Educators Association. She was inducted as an NASW Social Work Pioneer and named the American Public Health Association's Public Health Social Worker of the Year in 2020. Dr. Weaver has presented regionally, nationally, and internationally including at the UN. Her publications include *Explorations in Cultural Competence* (2005), *Social Issues in Contemporary Native America* (2014), *Trauma and Resilience in the Lives of Contemporary Native Americans* (2019), and the *Routledge International Handbook of Indigenous Resilience* (2022).

11

JESSICA HOPE

GRATITUDE AND METTLE

GOOD DAY,

I warmly welcome you to my chapter. If we were meeting in person, in true Southern fashion, I would offer you a drink of tea, Coke, water, or a grown-up beverage; we would get comfy and get started, so please do just that, if you are able.

When people ask what I do for work, I say, "I am a professional advocate." I am often in wonder and gratitude that my profession allows me to serve others with such breadth and a deep sense of impact and purpose. As a social worker, there is no shortage of difficult days, and I go back to gratitude, awe, and inspiration on my most challenging days. I work in JEDI, [cue Star Wars theme music here]. JEDI is an acronym for Justice (J), Equity (E), Diversity (D), and Inclusion (I). Several combinations are attempting to capture the expansiveness of this work; additional acronyms you may see are BIDE, DEI, VIBE, or D&I, with Belonging (B), and Value (V), sometimes added in variation[1]. I worked in this space before becoming an official social worker and before it became a societal buzzword.

Thanks to my parents, I have valued the sense of belonging since I was young. I was often first to stand up for a peer at recess. I spoke up in the boardroom as law enforcement officers around me spoke from their experienced but desensitized perspective. I have witnessed as a military unit including the leadership as they ostracized a rape victim for speaking up. I have also advised on process improvement involving sexual assault and domestic violence cases in the US Army. I have written about white privilege and how it shows up in data, marketing, and the like, and I currently consult a Fortune 100 company on its JEDI Strategy. However, the purpose of this book is to share *how* I arrived here. So, I am going to back up and we will meet back here later to discuss more about JEDI.

If you are already a social work practitioner, you may be making an eco-map or genogram in your head. If you are not, an ecomap is a visual tool we build to understand meaningful relationships with people, groups, and organizations. It helps us to conceptualize things like resources, types of connections, and energy/time received or given. It is often used together with the genogram to understand hereditary or familial patterns and how they are combined to influence the client or system we are evaluating.

Growing up, I did not have contact with my biological father as he was in prison.. We made contact later in my life when I was seventeen. I was raised by a single mother. My grandmother, an English professor, and my grandfather, a minister, had raised her. My mother worked as a nurse in an elderly-focused nursing home. I remember going with her to work during the night shift and sleeping in one of the beds. Sometimes, I would eat breakfast or dinner there, and with my mom's encouragement, I would talk and read my library books out loud to some of the residents. I loved to help in the kitchen preparing meals and, of course, eating cookies and Jell-O. I sensed the residents' appreciation of youth and their joy from even the most minor things as they asked me the details of my school day, friend dynamics, and playground games; they listened, and their eyes would sparkle with humor or reminiscing—of which, I couldn't be sure. Often, I felt their loneliness; it was a tactile empathy. My mother later transitioned into hospice nursing. She exposed me to the hushed and taboo topics of death, life-ending illness, family dynamics, euthanasia, legal rights, and how beautiful letting go can be. My mother has a palpable presence, a beautiful gift to this world, to be at a stranger's side as they pass away. Through her actions and values, she taught me not to shy away from hard things, and how to work hard and care for others.

My mother remarried when I was three, and I was wholly adopted into my Puerto Rican father's family. They never treated me differently for being a step kid but were often asked by outsiders who I was. My Dad is a first-generation mainlander, and from him, I learned about gratitude and conservation. In his own life of understanding scarcity, he imparted the value and wisdom of not wasting even the smallest things, such as finishing your plate or turning off a light when leaving the room. I didn't know the specifics or the why until I was older, but my father infused a deep sense of respect for others regardless of their appearance or who they are and to stand up for someone when they cannot stand up for themselves. I watched him step in when a homeless man was being bullied. The bullies were three young men who bore the look of 'being caught,' and ashamed, embarrassed, craven at their behavior, they ran immediately. He spoke to me about it afterward, and it took a few rounds of conversation as new questions arose in my brain and heart, but we got through it. My Dad spoke to me like I could stand up for others like he had done, even if I were small, a girl, or outnumbered. Later in my life, I learned that he had a rare disease called Perthes Disease, and had spent several years of his childhood in a wheelchair. When he arrived in the mainland US, he taught himself English and opened a computer business. He taught me about perseverance, being a lifelong learner, and gratitude. One of the most important things he showed me was that your diagnosis doesn't own you. It is merely a sliver of your life story.

It never felt like I chose to be an advocate or a social worker; it is in my DNA, my way of being, and as much a part of me as the fingers typing on this keyboard and the heart beating in my chest. I don't know the exact delineation of nature versus nurture on this topic; nevertheless, my parents hold a profound influence, and I am eternally grateful to them for their examples.

Rather than focus on the woes of moving frequently, I choose optimism. My school years consisted of frequent moves. I stayed as involved as I could in extracurricular activities like track, cross country, cheerleading, volleyball, basketball, swimming, choir, debate, and so on, depending on where we lived. High school was merely something to 'get through' so I could travel, learn, and live life.

I am thankful for the practice of introducing myself, getting to know new people, being fine with being uncomfortable, and the learned ability to navigate new situations. I have stood up for someone on the playground or in the hallway, meeting room, or parking lot more than once. It is never easy. Not one iota of it is easy, but it is a hell of a lot better than the feelings that result from just walking past a situation. I am not speaking of stepping into a trivial argument that school-age students tend to inflate. I am speaking of listening to the gut intuition that something is not right, and taking action or saying something. I joined the United States Army between my high school junior and senior years to pay for college, and left for bootcamp shortly after graduation. I had teachers, church members, and acquaintances try to talk me out of serving. They were uneasy about a young woman joining the service, about deployments and safety, but I barely heard their concerns.

My military experience is a combination of highs and lows. From day one of my military services, it was a struggle. I don't mean the challenge of physical fitness and regimented schedules that is a normal part of serving in the military. I am referring to the unexpected struggle of discrimination, gender-related and then some; women being treated as less worthy of being a soldier or less deserving of opportunities than men. I joined when these gender disparities were shifting conversations within the Army. I have seen many changes in policy, culture, and opportunity for women in my twenty years of service, but there are still significant opportunities to lessen the disparity gap. I believe that my life experiences up to that point gave me the resolve to survive in the most discriminatory, sexist, racist, 'boys' club', classist organization I have ever, to this day, been a part of. These discriminatory practices were more often subtle nuances and microaggressions rather than blatant actions. It took me a while to be able to name them once I was out of survival mode. I know from my male comrades that my experience as a woman was very different than theirs, even as we shared being enlisted service members and decorated soldiers. I have had some incredible mentors and leaders in my career in both men and women. I hold out hope that the culture changes for the better at the boots on ground level that extends beyond policies.

I raised my hand for every school and training I could and had the opportunity to serve as an expert advisor in Equal Opportunity, Suicide Intervention, Sexual Assault Advocacy, as well as various physically demanding training opportunities. I went to Airborne School, a physically demanding and rigorous training course with an approximate

75% attrition rate, where soldiers learn how to parachute out of aircraft. I was one of two women to graduate in my cohort. At that time, the push for equal opportunity and climate of respect and dignity were not nearly what is strived for today in the Armed Forces. At that school, I was asked daily "whose dick I had sucked to get into training." It was the norm for myself and the women around me.

I joined the service primarily to obtain educational assistance. It was not easy to have an inconsistent, full-time job schedule, attend school, and have a family, and I fought to make it work as best as possible. My first duty assignment was overseas, and when college classes were offered, I signed up as soon as possible. I went to school during lunch, evenings, or weekends. Overseas, professors tried to accommodate our unpredictable military schedules; I remember sitting in class trying to stay awake after forty hours of duty and no sleep. The Army offered college courses, but that doesn't mean they made it easy or even supported it. Looking back, I would call it tolerance. We received no accommodation in scheduling or mission assignments when enrolled in college classes. To sum up a long journey, after repeating many classes due to 'withdraw due to military duty,' I ended up completing my Bachelor of Psychology degree after ten years and with no monetary debt. Debt can be measured not only in dollars and cents, but also in the physical toll that stress, a busy schedule, and a high energy career takes on one's health. It took me ten years to finish college; in that time, I had been promoted several times ahead of my peers, moved four times around the country, gotten married, had a child, and experienced two of the most profoundly significant, life-altering events of my life.

First, I underwent open-heart surgery while pregnant due to a medical error. I had—and still have—no rights due to a law known as the Feres Doctrine that prohibits members of the Armed Forces from suing the government for malpractice, injury, negligence, death, etc. Second, I was sexually assaulted. There is no shortage of public coverage on how the military has astonishingly blundered this issue and displayed a pattern of blatant negligence. I am one of many survivors who have never received justice or closure. In the military, you can choose to report unrestricted or restricted. Restricted means that there will not be an investigative process triggered, but you can still receive certain types of support. Unrestricted initiates the investigative process. I had seen too many times the retaliation and reputation of being a "problem child" slapped on so many victims who filed unrestricted reports; I chose not to seek unrestricted assistance until a significant time after the assault. These two events on their own are life-altering and traumatic, but to have two significant events occur in such proximity was an intensity beyond which I have the words to articulate, even to this day. I decided to leave the Army as an active-duty Soldier, and I became an Army Reserve member while in recovery.

Throughout school, I just *knew* I wanted to be a psychiatrist. I had already applied to medical school, but the infinite wisdom of our collegiate professors in my senior year changed that trajectory for me. Our capstone project was to have an informational interview with three to five professionals in our area of interest. I interviewed psychiatrists, psychologists, social workers, life coaches, and marriage counselors. My MD and Ph.D. interviewees shared their burnout experiences. They felt it was challenging to serve their profession in another capacity because of the niche they had developed within a specific patient clientele. I learned that social work allows more flexibility in what I wanted to practice and is not confined to neat little columns and rows like other close professions. The foundations of social work education would prepare me for a myriad of options. When my interviewees turned the tables and asked me what I had been up to or wanted to do when I grew up, my response invoked the same feedback from them…"Jessica, go into social work."

I didn't choose Justice, Equity, Diversity, and Inclusion (JEDI) specifically. I merged into JEDI work due to the aggregation of my experience, educational opportunities, and real-world application of these opportunities combined with my passion for advocacy. Very few of my fellow JEDI practitioners are social workers. They come from all walks of life and educational backgrounds. They teach me every day, and I am humbled and grateful to have them as my peers; I hope that I reciprocate. Every day, through our successes, milestones, tears, empathy, exasperation, and motivation, I and my fellow practitioners choose JEDI. Social workers, in particular, have been primed since the beginning of our educational journey to think from the JEDI perspective. JEDI is not a new endeavor in our society, and this space has always been emotionally charged. Still, only in recent years have citizens, families, employees, employers, and leaders opened up to having these conversations more broadly. The death of George Floyd brought these conversations to a head and catalyzed a movement across the globe. Even if JEDI is not your specific focus, you will now find yourself intertwining concepts of JEDI into yourself, your clients, and your everyday work processes.

I love our profession because we can apply your social work, academic, and life experience towards a broad range of interests. We recognize and acknowledge the benefits of the diversity of experience. Our resumes welcome evidence-based practice, research, volunteer work, formal clinician hours, supervisory roles, policy advisors and change-makers, infinite non-profit opportunities, international action, and even how all of these intersect with other areas. Social workers have the flexibility to work at the micro, mezzo, or macro level. Microwork focuses on individuals, mezzo works with small groups, and macro with large populations, programs, and policies. JEDI is woven into the fabric at each of these levels. This work is so crucial that I donate my time to mentor and advise on JEDI, women veterans' issues, and other topics I am passionate about. I counsel how to turn JEDI commitments into data-informed, measurable, realistic actions that are planned for an incremental and maintainable change.

From my perspective, the most rewarding part of this work is when someone has the psychological and emotional safety to break from prejudicial and biased thinking and be open to a new way of viewing things. They lean into their discomfort and smash through a stereotype. I find the most joy when I see these revelations joining together for a culture shift that we observe in the data. When humans feel welcome to come as they are into an environment, being afforded the same opportunities as those around them with their contributions acknowledged and valued, we see the benefits come to fruition evidenced by data. Normal practice is for advocacy, data analysis, culture, human capital, social work, employee health and wellness to work in silos, but I have shown how these merge together in my JEDI methodology.

I hope you leave this book and my shared journey knowing you can find joy, meaningful work, significance, love of the profession, and quality of life on your unique path; that you and the experiences that built you are valuable. You can practice resilience beyond trauma, and you do not have to be your diagnosis or history or trauma. You can choose again, start again, and grow again.

Justice (J), Equity (E), Diversity (D), Inclusion (I), Belonging (B), Value (V)

Pearl of Wisdom

"I wish for you the practice of humanity,
the knowing that we are each capable of growth,
the courage to change and allow others to change,
and the grace to meet people where they are rather than where you want them to be
and above all. Be a nice human."
~ Jessica Hope

The views expressed in this article are those of the author and do
not reflect the official policy or position of the Department of
Defense or the U.S. Government

ABOUT THE AUTHOR

Jessica Hope leads with extreme ownership, fierce belief in the goodness of others, and saying hard things with love. Her breadth of work spans from National policy influence, local government planning, and a myriad of corporate, military, and non-profit experience.

She is a Diversity, Equity, and Inclusion practitioner. Jessica uses data and evidence-based practices, focused on measurable outcomes, to hold leaders accountable and influence change for equality in the corporate world. Mrs. Hope concurrently serves as a senior people leader in the Army Reserves, where she has been a Suicide Intervention Specialist, Equal Opportunity and Sexual Assault Advocate since 2002. She councils on how these issues intersect with military leadership, culture, resiliency, and wellness.

Jessica holds a Master's degree in Advanced Generalist Social Work from IUPUI. She further expands the conversation into the disparities of poverty as a Certified Financial Social Worker.

LinkedIn: linkedin.com/in/jessica-hope-people-leader

12

DANIEL MARTIN, CHILD WELFARE INNOVATOR

A CONSCIENCE AND COURAGE

"Why did you do all this for me?" Wilbur asked. "I don't deserve it. I've never done anything for you." "You have been my friend," replied Charlotte. "That in itself is a tremendous thing." — (White, 1952)

"How do you want people to feel when reading this book, if you contribute?" My immediate thought? I want them to feel the need to do different. Could sharing my story about child welfare encourage that in any way? I often think about how I came to social work and child welfare and the lessons learned. There is more that those outside the field and those touched by it could ever know.

At the same time, I believe there is much that those in the field know, but maybe are operating in safety and hesitant to acknowledge. And, if they do, they do so in silence. Silence is lonely. And loneliness can kill.

Cindy Blackstock speaks of Indigenous people's experience of child welfare and the need for "moral courage in child protection and in the child welfare field as a contrast to moral cowardice, which diminishes children" (Blackstock, 2011). So powerful. I mean, one would think this concept may motivate a "courageous" response. And I thought…child welfare would benefit from a conscience and some courage.

I thought, "Stories hold the power of truth…of lived experience. The lesson for us all being…?"

Pay attention to people's stories and those who tell them.

Here's a bit of mine.

I was born in Ontario, Canada to parents who worked harder and carried a level of stress neither I nor my siblings ever truly knew until older; we didn't comprehend it in real time. They gave us a foundation built on unconditional love. Don't get me wrong: there were challenges, struggles, and times where we didn't quite get the underlying reasons why. In that, they protected us from the true stressors. I still don't know how they got four kids six years apart to baseball games and practices all summer long. And skating and pastel classes, basketball, and school sports of every kind, and scouts and girl guides. Heck, mom even coached ball for a couple years.

Dad delivered furniture for a large retail chain, as did our grandad before him. (Me too, as summer work, which meant Dad would carry the freezer or couch...while carrying me.) He taught us work ethic and loyalty and treated each person whose home we entered with kindness. He was the gentlest of men.

Mom took care of the homefront and all our needs. Doing so with limited amenities, only occasional access to a vehicle, and in the relative isolation of a tiny neighborhood on a country road, she was the family quarterback. She called all the plays, making sure that as we grew, we didn't grow away from each other. Family holidays were non-negotiable. Relationships mattered. And we all remain better for it. They instilled the value of family and relationships early and often, and of taking care of one another. We miss them both so dearly.

While there are many memories, one epitomizes who they were and the lifelong impact they left. In my early forties during a particularly difficult time, I sat weeping. Both Mom and Dad were sitting quietly. And Dad said in the softest of voices, "When you were little, I could just pick you up and dust you off," not realizing that in those words, he and they together, just did.

And they sat with me.

Everyone needs and should have someone to sit with them.

I knew nothing of social work nor child welfare at all. We visited a teenage family member in a home that was not her own where other young people lived. It seemed unusual and I felt for her; it seemed lonely. It didn't make sense, nor did why mom and dad took us there to visit. All we knew is they did because it was right. And it was.

Everyone needs someone to care.

I graduated high school, dreaming of becoming a baseball player. Encouraged to follow my dreams, I attended a West Georgia Junior College camp where, as a Canadian I learned a) you must learn to chew tobacco at an early age and b) never eat pizza and chocolate milk the night before your first day on a hot Georgia baseball field. Ball wasn't meant to be. I took a year off school delivering building materials, "tried" university the next year, then went back to building supplies to ultimately take a job in construction framing houses.

Then, something happened. It was a call to switch directions that at the time was just a whole lotta hurt! I fell off a roof, through wooden trusses and onto wooden framed walls, and hit the concrete floor. I injured everything: fractured my skull, lost my sense of taste and smell, pervasive head pain, many a physical break and trauma that would last my lifetime.

From there, I became a client. In an efficient case management machine, I became a case. I was hospitalized for weeks on the neurological ward, followed by intensive physiotherapy, back clinic, strength training, memory loss, and even counseling to learn how to eat. The goal? Rehab and get off the system. Whose goal? Well, I was motivated and the system sure was. The problem? My body wasn't.

I learned to be a "good client." One who appreciates and is indebted to the service, to get support I learned I had a right to either way. When the system decided after vocational aptitude testing that I should be a dairy farmer (huh?), electrocardiograph technician, or a social service worker, they signed me up to be a technician. It was the shortest, cheapest course.

I wanted to go to university. They said, "From a construction framer to university?" and laughed out loud. They decided *my* path and controlled writing *my* future chapters. It was devastating.

Do not write others' future chapters. Give others the pen to write their own.

Over time, I learned how to respond to the system's barriers, having others close to me advocate and teach me how to find advocacy within. I relied on a network. So, in spite of the machine, I registered for university, achieving A's in first year psychology and sociology and returned to them, grades in hand, saying "Yes I can. This is how. I am capable. Please support me." And they agreed to support a 3-year BA. I had proven my *value* and was assessed as *deserving*. Weeks later, I got off an elevator on the wrong floor. The sign read, "Social Work". I read a pamphlet and thought, "This!" I had two prerequisites, saw I would need a combined degree, mapped out a way to do 5 years of school in 3.5 years, and pitched to the efficient machine, convincing them I would be more employable. And as I proved I did as mapped, the more support and less surveillance I received. The good client. That was me. This was my way into Social Work.

I graduated at the top of my class with a couple of awards, but with the very same piece of paper those beside me had. I applied to many jobs and landed a contract in child welfare within weeks. The good client was a client no more.

Never dismiss capability.

"The Hammer and the Helper"

I wish I'd known when entering child welfare how politicized it is. I didn't know until later the systems seemed designed in a manner that professionalizes relationships in hierarchy and creates dependencies. These are referred to as concepts in social work curriculum, but not made real. Maybe it was my own naivety, but it seemed to conflict with humanity and interfered with the role of a family's own important people.

I worked hard to become a "good worker", just as I was a good client before, and acquiesced to the system's demands. I studied relevant laws, regulations, and standards, and focused on meeting standard time frames, or else I would be "out of compliance." I thought this meant I would not be providing good service. I didn't recognize how hard I was working, to sustain the system. It came at a cost to my family as well as the families "served."

I left one organization for another; it paid better. I had a son now and needed to provide. I worked after hours ten to twelve nights per month. One night while reading to my son Steven, then 4, my pager went off, and he responded, "Daddy, I hate the beeper." It was the tiny machine that *took me away from him.*

In child welfare, we were taught to balance helping with authority. It was affectionately called the "hammer and the helper." At the time, I didn't ask why we needed the hammer. I assumed they knew better, as seasoned veterans of this complex system of laws, rules, and regulations. And I learned to believe in "experts" on other people's lives, and didn't think, "Who is the expert on your life, Dan? And who should that be?"

One evening, years ago on after-hours, I was told I needed to get a pre-drafted warrant to remove a newborn baby. I secured the warrant, and with police at either side of me, I executed it. "Executed." The mother asked me in tears, "But why?" And in that moment, in doing what I was told, I, dumbfounded, answered, "I don't know. It is what I was directed to do." And my stomach ached. Imagine the pain she must have felt.

My efforts as a "good worker" serving the system over time were recognized; I became a supervisor. A promotion! Sit with those few last sentences for a moment. I have, since, for years.

Most days I raced home, teetering on late, still not having done enough, and with that stomach-ache. What I did or didn't do didn't seem to matter in families' lives. I tried hard, behaved with kindness and effort towards being least intrusive, and most supportive as I could. In the end, I am not sure it helped when I had a hammer in my pocket. It took far too long to truly reflect on that.

A few years back, I heard something that resonated deeply. Molly McGrath Tierney in her influential Ted Talk, said, "Oppression is a tricky devil: it gets good people to unwittingly pick up its weapons and use them in the name of helping when we have the best of intentions in our heart." (McGrath Tierney, 2014). Did this define what I had become "good at?"

Learn early; reflect often.

A conscience is "a guide to the rightness or wrongness of one's behavior" (Merriam-Webster, 2021). I needed one, as relationships in this child protection role were centered in power and seemed to correspond with my tummy aches. Adversity, you see, has an impact on health. Do not forget that. Also, remember Dr. Gabor Mate's wisdom that, "Safety is not the absence of threat; it is the presence of connection". Connection buffers adversity. We are safer in relationship. It all interconnects, for us and those we serve. The thing is that in line of our work? We remove connection.

I increased my attention to the research, outcomes for children in care and families in service, including across generations. And stories. I increasingly listened to the stories. Not the story told "in file," but the person, the youth. And here is what they said.

"It…. doesn't… work!! We are the experts, as we live the outcomes of what you do, and guess what? It doesn't work and it's hurting us. You figured out how to do it this way and do it. So, you can figure out how to do it differently and do that. And lastly if you want to do it right? Ask us. We know. And we are happy to tell you. But know this first; don't ask us to tell you if you aren't going to do something about it. We are experts in many things; one being in disappointment. And we don't want any more…"

What they said was to grow a conscience that guides you toward rightness. Then follow it.

You can't unknow what you know. So, either live with it (and the associated stomach-aches) or do something about it.

A conscience was a start but must be followed by the courage to act. Acting can be difficult, particularly alone in a system, where you too are without connection and hence possibly unsafe. Remember, loneliness can kill.

There is vulnerability required in stepping outside the box because our conscience—and statistics, research, and those we serve—tell us we cannot ignore the outcomes anymore. We need to shift from that place of vulnerability to one of courageousness. To a place that shows initiative based on lessons learned, founded in science that tells us that what we do in the name of helping people in fact is destructive to their health. And concurrently it can be harmful to the health of those providing the service (see stomach-aches). It takes some reconciling to acknowledge that prescriptive practice leads to repeating the same mistakes every day in the name of policy. It takes telling the truth.

In my work now with HEERO (Helping Everyone/Each other Reach Out), the longest served youth in care across North America have taught me that we need to be vulnerable together to shift to collective courageousness. It's what youth in the HEERO process do. They help each other to know they are worthy of different and better and that they are capable. They support each other to take risks to reconnect with their people and communities to whom they "belong" where previously they were alone and separated in service from family, friends, neighbors, community, and each other.

It takes the system "giving up control" or a taking-back on the part of families to write their own chapters. We need to shift from playing expert roles on others' lives to one of bringing their communities together to support and help one another; resourced on the outside by the state so that family systems in communities can build or rebuild, reconnect, and thrive. We must embrace the diversity and uniqueness of every family and resist the inclination toward prescription. We need to help families define their needs and for them to define their plan; not us. And activate "their people" to help them from a place of what they *can* do. Because they are capable. They have people who love or can love them. We need to begin to see and welcome them. We need to expect different from the system, including becoming welcoming to family and friends. Because therein lies the strength to help families in difficulty.

This is core to what I believe is necessary for a change in the way of serving. We need to move away from this lens of surveillance, isolation, and authority to one of collective and community-wide healing/well-being, away from a place of authority to a place of walking with. And importantly, a place of recognizing the capabilities of all. A place of seeing solutions within families and their networks and supporting friendships. Not stopping them with rules or conditions. A place… without hammers.

If alone is powerless, together is powerful.

In August 2018, I had chest pains. My doctor, sufficiently concerned, referred me to the Emergency Department. They determined it may be my heart. I would need an angiogram. It was Friday and these were not done over the weekend, so I was admitted.

We had three young children, a baby and a six and seven-year-old who played soccer on Saturdays on separate teams; my wife and I were the coaches. With that and so many other demands to meet, I had to be home. I explained to the doctor that being admitted interfered with being a Dad and a partner so proposed to the doctor to sign myself out until Monday. Let's just say she said, "No".

I talked to my wife and thought, "Wait…I have a brother and sisters, brothers and sisters-in-law, an older son…" From vulnerability to courage, I called my brother who said, "We got this". One would take care of the baby; others would accompany my wife to soccer. My brother and sister-in-law would drive my vehicle home, my older son would visit and bring my things, and my daughter Emily, offered emotional support from far away. My maternal brother and sister-in-law would help Jen at home, and Grandma and Grandpa would come later. They assembled a plan, and my stress was buffered by their support.

And they sat with me.

Relationships are critical to human health and well-being. Having them all taken? Devastating.

If the removal of a child leads to an indescribable loneliness and life/body-altering pain; if removal means they not only lose their mom and or dad, but their grandparents, extended family, neighbors, coaches, teachers, schoolmates, friends, their soccer team with the purple shirts and #8 on the back and all they identified with as a team-mate, and their faith communities and camp counselors; instead of these being adversity and losses, why can't they be the strength. The solutions instead? And, in times of need, why can't the call be to them? They just may answer and say, "We got this."

Ask yourself, what would I want to happen were it me? Then do that; with a conscience and courage.

To those in systems deciding who youth can have contact with: let them decide. Maintain relationships for them. Support them to welcome family and friends, just as you would your own.

Thank you Raven, Alicia, Mirela, Damien, Shayne, and all young people who have graced me with your kindness and wisdom beyond your years. You are the best teachers.

Pearl of Wisdom
"To all: Pay attention to people's stories and those who tell them. Everyone needs and should have someone to sit with them. Their people exist! Let that be your work."
~ Daniel Martin

ABOUT THE AUTHOR

Dan graduated Summa Cum Laude from McMaster University in Hamilton, Ontario, in Social Work in 1994 and has over 25 years of human service experience. This includes working for 4 different Child Welfare agencies in Ontario, Canada, in front line, supervisory and managerial capacities across all functions. In addition, he has worked in the Youth and Adult Mental Health and Addictions Sectors serving both children and adults in various capacities including program management. Dan developed and trains the HEERO™ (Helping Everyone/Each Other Reach Out) approach and is focused on moving it forward in both Canada and the U.S.A and further internationally.

Website: www.HEERO.ca
LinkedIn: http://linkedin.com/in/daniel-martin-65b006155
Facebook Page: HEERO

13

DR. SUJEETA E. MENON, PH.D., LMSW

SOCIAL WORK IS A JOURNEY AND A CALLING

I WAS BORN of Indian descent in the early 1980's and lived in Singapore for most of my life until I moved to Houston, Texas in 2016. There, I pursued my Master's and Ph.D. in Social Work at the Graduate College of Social Work at the University of Houston. I am a Singaporean Indian female. My father was born in Kerala and moved to Singapore with his whole family when he was nine years old. My mother was born in Singapore. Singaporeans experience a conglomeration of different ethnicities, languages, and cultures in one place. Singapore embraces multicultural diversity and unity like no other country. English and Mandarin are the most spoken languages. This played a significant role as I was growing into a social worker, as I sought to learn the local languages to better connect with the local population and better 'fit in' with society.

Growing up in Singapore presented multiple levels of influence. Singapore is often referred to as a small red dot, yet it is a mighty economic power force that rose to its success in a significantly short time. Since fifty-seven years ago, this multi-cultural city now boasts a robust education system, a stable political government, and a thriving workforce. There is a culture of building success that became a prerequisite to life. For me, this early upbringing also felt like a pressure cooker. There was a drive to achieve, and you either fall in or you fall out. Living in a stressful environment came with high expectations and disappointments, but also came with achievement and success—for those who made the cut! My early years were focused on academics, getting full scores on every test (which I didn't!), and being tutored for my weaker subjects. Not long after, I found that I was unable to roll with the pressures and expectations, so I fell out of course. At twelve, I found myself struggling to pass my Cambridge examinations and found myself in an extended secondary school program that gave me an extra year in school. Surely that did nothing positive for my self-esteem, even though it gave me one more year to get through my "O" levels Cambridge examinations at the age of seventeen. In this season of my life, I crossed each hurdle by the grace of God, support of my family, and my church community. It sure took a village to get me to where I am today. Through my upbringing, I also learned the value in helping others. I started mentoring youth from my church in Singapore when I was sixteen, and it gave me great joy and delight. My mother also often mentored young kids through teaching. There was nothing else I wanted to do but to walk alongside others who were struggling to find their fit in society and purpose in life. What would that look like? What, who, where, when, and HOW? I had never heard about social work before I entered college.

There was a life path formula for each of us that was utilized in every household: finish school, go to college, get a good-paying job, get married, and have children. It was hard to deviate from the formula. Hence, we followed the prescribed pathway to reach our destination of success, or rather, society's view of success. This pathway was fraught with rocks, slopes, debris, and sharp turns. My academic ability was tested due to an attention deficit disorder. It was challenging to even complete reading a book, or be patient enough to solve a mathematics equation. The only way was to *deal with it*. And so, I dealt with it by finding my own way within the prescribed way. Along the way, I had multiple tutors, caring adults, and supportive teachers along with my family to nudge me through and believe in me. The very reason why I often play that role now to the young girls I work with is that hope can keep the dream alive when others believe in you. My parents spent a lot of money on tutoring and academic help by sending me to learning camps, hoping that I could get to the end of the path. I was given every opportunity possible to succeed academically. Making it to the National

University of Singapore seemed an impossible dream, but I knew I could do it. I often remembered the Bible verse, "With God, all things are possible" (Luke 1:37), and that God had a "purpose for me and a plan for me" (Jeremiah 29:11). So now, I was one step closer to the destination of success, but I was clueless as to what I needed to study to get me to that destination.

It is hard to imagine that someone who started as a lower-performing student would even step foot into a top-tier university. My early struggles at Paya Lebar Methodist Girls Primary and Secondary School where I spent eleven years of my life created a strong, resilient spirit in me that helped me to push away all obstacles in my pathway to reach that destination. The formative years were crucial to character and faith-building as they shaped me into who I am today. The Christian school environment was a great balance of support and rigor, and was also where I formed my spiritual beliefs. The opportunity to take exposure classes in my first semester in college allowed me to find my passion and the closest alignment to my heart's calling. Little did I realize that social work would emerge as the only course of study that I wanted to pursue. What started as an exploration turned into my life-long profession!

It was hard to imagine what my career would look like until college scholarship applications came around. I obtained a community-based social work training scholarship which placed me in a non-profit. Soon, I found myself signing on the dotted line to receive the scholarship and work for Methodist Welfare Services Tampines Family Service Center as my designated place of employment for a minimum of one year. In hindsight, I guess that was easy; I didn't need to worry about employment. The next five years at this non-profit planted the social work foundation that I am still grateful to have. Sometimes something unexpected happens when you're not looking for it!

Starting my career as a social worker in Singapore at the age of twenty-five came with multiple ups and downs. I remember I felt so conscious of my youth as I worked with older adults, couples, parents, and the schools. I often tried to dress more maturely or adorn a fake ring just to find my own fit with my clients and to be taken seriously as a professional Social Worker. Much later, I learned the term was "imposter syndrome": the experience of feeling incompetent and being afraid to be called out as a fraud. This term was first coined in the 1970's by psychologists Suzanna Imes and Pauline Rose Clance, who developed this theory in relevance to women who are high-achieving yet self-sabotage through doubt and overcompensation. Because of my tendency to constantly self-reflect, I've identified that this could have been caused by the pursuit of perfectionism, where I set high yet unrealistic expectations, only to find out that I had to push myself to the brink of burnout to achieve them. Living in a highly driven society with high expectations could also have contributed to this feeling that I would never be good enough. In social work, this presents a greater issue: people often think of us as superheroes, as we seek to change the world. Hence, it is imperative to develop a strong sense of community among co-workers, a supportive supervisor, professional development, and a work-life balance. I also voluntarily joined the Executive Committee at the Singapore Association of Social Workers for six years, which offered me the opportunity to advocate for social workers, better quality standards in care, accreditation, and to celebrate Social Workers' achievements. This exposure honed my networking and administrative skills as I learned to communicate and work alongside other social workers in the field. There is a common saying that you have to cross the three-year mark to stay the long haul in social work. I attest this to be true, as it took me close to three years to find my groove, manage my internal and external expectations of myself, to develop professionally through training, and to manage myself emotionally as I work with clients who had experienced trauma, loss, and unfortunate circumstances.

My desire to work with young people started when I was sixteen as a youth ministry leader in my church for many years. It is my belief that the opportunity to explore working with different types of clients further reinforced my passion to work with young people. The initial exposure also offered me a deeper understanding of the systems that we work with. Every young person has a family, a school, a possible religious affiliation, or a peer network, and it is critical to have a wide range of micro-skills to address the needs of various subpopulations. This initial exposure made me a well-rounded social worker, with a depth of knowledge concerning complex presenting issues and the interaction between systems. It took me five years of being overworked and underpaid to reach a serious stage of burnout, and I realized that I needed a change of work environment.

After leaving my first job, I had to recharge, re-calibrate, and rest. That took me on a long backpacking trip to South America for six weeks, where I visited Argentina, Peru, Chile, and Brazil with two of my girlfriends. This experience took me out of my comfort zone, exposed me to a different world, and helped me to reevaluate my professional career and personal goals. I entered into a new season that offered me new possibilities, new thinking, and big decisions on my next steps towards my long-term goals. I decided to work for the Singapore Courts as a court social worker where I mediated between divorcing parents to uphold the best interest of their children. While it was an important role of social work, it was too brief and task-focused for long-term impact. I quickly discovered that this job was not meant for me and left after three months after a call from my first boss. I was given the opportunity to take up a new managerial role to direct a small group home for young women aged sixteen to twenty-one. I found myself back on my journey to find my passion. However, moving from a social worker to a Senior Social Worker to a Head of Center was a large leap. A leap of work responsibilities, and a leap of faith. After only six years, I found myself having to start a whole new group home where the clients would stay with us for up to a year to complete their probation orders. This was a new yet innovative service that would prevent them from entering the prison system at a vulnerable age. As a thirty-year-old, I became the house mama to fifteen to twenty beautiful girls each time, developed a therapeutic milieu and programs for them to thrive, created school and work opportunities, parent engagement, mentorship, scholarship opportunities, and offered spiritual support. I managed a staff team of twelve along with social work interns. This experience was life-altering. It was only through this experience that I was able to find authenticity as a social worker, truly empathize with their life stories, and fully engage in their pain and their victories. Despite being the toughest round-the-clock job, I gained more from it than I could ever imagine. It was such a privilege to journey with these young women. At the four-year mark, I was privy to the girls' reentry and post-care as well, which threw me for a loop. Our girls did so well in structure with us, but once they were independent, it was different. I kept asking myself what it would take for them to desist from crime. Little did I realize that this question I held in 2015 would become my research question for my PhD in 2017.

Through this tough job, I was also in a new relationship. During this time, I received immense love and support from my husband in our long-distance relationship between Singapore and Malaysia, and this was also one of the factors that kept me resilient in this role. I offered 100% of myself to this role, which could not continue once we were married. I realized that some jobs are designed for your life stage, while others are not. It was then that we made the tough decision to leave Singapore and start our experience in America.

In 2016, my husband and I decided to move to Houston, Texas. We became full-time students once again. We started our married life together in a new city with a new community and as new mature students. While this may sound tough, it was made easier by finding a strong church community at City of Refuge and the Intervarsity Christian Fellowship on campus. After a year and a half, both of us graduated. However, I had the same lingering question: "What does it take for young women to desist from crime?" I knew that I had to embark on a Ph.D. program to answer this question. After giving birth to our beautiful daughter in 2017, I continued my academic journey till 2021, where I had the privilege of working with esteemed professors and researchers all around the country. With the support of my Ph.D. department at the University of Houston, I was exposed to literature that slowly answered my question. I carved out my own study and had the benefit of working on the local probation data to answer these questions as well. My Ph.D. became my full circle moment. I had worked in this field for so long with that same question, and it was finally answered. And the answer to my question was simple: it takes love, understanding, and a whole village to support a young woman's desistance from crime. I already knew this from before. But what I didn't know is that we are surrounded by systems that marginalize and oppress our young girls, that perpetuate their trauma and unfortunate adverse childhood experiences, which then pose barriers to their successful re-entry. Systems work is macro work, and this finding put me into a nice balance of micro and macro intervention to effect change. This led to my first big grant-writing endeavor to fund a gender-specific intervention program known as VOICES for justice-involved girls in Houston.

In 2019, I was employed as a Risk Assessment Specialist by Change Happens!, a local non-profit in the Third Ward, Houston, Texas. This was a huge opportunity to work with local youth in the schools where I would provide brief assessments and intervention. This fifteen-month exposure opened my eyes to truly appreciate the struggles, challenges, and resilience of our young people. This work invigorated my commitment to social, economic, and racial justice. I had discovered that our assessment tools were not racially sensitive or representative, which urged me to expand our tools to include racially specific questions on the Adverse Childhood Experiences survey. We collected data for five hundred students which helped us to identify the need to include different types of adversity such as racial discrimination, bullying, witnessing violence, and suicide. Working for a non-profit that is evidence and data-driven was truly a blessing. As a Ph.D. candidate, having on-the-ground experience and an aptitude for research was a whole new skill set that I acquired in this season. I started to value the importance of being data-driven and evidence-based, rather than going with the flow (although this is important sometimes!). In my journey with social work, I have always created and developed new programs or services. This prompted me to create a new program with new lenses for the population that I've always been passionate to work with. My greatest support came from my CEO, Ms. Helen Stagg, a grant-writing guru, who encouraged me to take the leap and write. The program was funded in 2020 and helped over one hundred girls in its first year. One year later, I embarked on my second big grant-writing endeavor, to expand the program to young boys as well. This new program also received federal funding in 2021. These successful endeavors remind me that we can always dream and imagine, and when you are ready to make your dream a reality, you will find the support you need to make it happen. My daughter always grounds me to be focused on making this world a better place. Recently, I launched my children's book, *I'm a Social Worker: Let's Learn to Advocate,* based on a true story that she encountered in school. My sixteen years of social work experience along with being a mother culminated in this moment where I felt immense joy to teach young children about diversity, equity, and advocacy at the same time. Children deserve to know about this wonderful profession before college, so they can be inspired to help others at a young age.

From a bird's eye view, I can confidently say that every little experience I've had in my social work journey has brought me to this point. Every client I've worked with has enriched my global views and perspectives about people and about social work. Every client's journey has sowed seeds into my own social work journey, where my end goal is always to be the best version of myself and the best Social Worker I can be. With this goal, I'm excited to see how the rest of my social work journey unfolds.

Pearl of Wisdom
"Your social work journey is unique to you, live out your calling and let your journey enrich you one step at a time"
~ Dr. Sujeeta E. Menon

ABOUT THE AUTHOR

Dr. Sujeeta Elizabeth Menon, 39, was born in Singapore, where she found her love for social work. After working for 10 years as a Social worker, she moved to Houston, TX to pursue her MSW and PhD In social work from the University of Houston Graduate College of Social Work. Prior to graduating in May 2021, she developed a girls empowerment program known as VOICES at Change Happens!, a non profit located in the third ward, Houston TX. She is now the program coordinator for the program, as she continues to partake in research that supports the reentry of justice involved young women. Sujeeta continues to spread her love for social work by adjunct teaching at different colleges. She is also a children's book author for the *"I'm a Social Worker"* book series.

LinkedIn: linkedin.com/in/sujeetaelizabethmenon/

14

NICOLE YOUNG, LCSW, LCADC

A CALLING FOR CONNECTION

"INVISIBLE THREADS ARE THE STRONGEST TIES."

- Nietzsche

As a little girl I dreamed of being a garbologist. Yes, you read that right. I found trash fascinating and wanted to study the environment. To their credit, I don't remember my parents laughing at me. As I got older, I toyed with becoming a lawyer; mostly because my family said I never stopped talking and I could argue better than the grown-ups. I would set up all my stuffed animals and argue in front of them as if I were in court. I could listen to the sound of my own voice for days, and my parents can attest to that. I always knew I would go to college, despite the absence of a single college graduate several generations deep. My father had dropped out of high school after my grandfather died unexpectedly to work and help my grandmother. Education was simply not valued as strongly as work was valued.

My parents are the salt of the earth kind of people. Both encompass a work ethic I have always marveled over. I like to think that some of it rubbed off on me. I have never seen either of them take a sick day and we didn't do vacations in my home. My father, the youngest of six siblings, always lamented that you "go to work, be grateful you have a job to go to, and you go to work." My father has been a truck driver in some capacity my whole life. He is 71 years old and still gets up before the sun, puts on his work boots and heads out the door. It was a routine that gave me great comfort as a child. My mother spent the largest part of her working life as a school bus driver. I used to love going with her to the bus yard and playing on the equipment I wasn't supposed to touch. I loved how it smelled of diesel, dirt, and burnt coffee. I remember being in awe of her ability to drive that 40-foot machine up a snowy hill or turn it around on a street with cars on both sides. She oozed confidence and calm, and I believe that seeped into my pores.

I am the youngest of three children, however the age gap is great enough that, in birth order studies, I am considered an only child. When I was in kindergarten, my sister was learning to drive and my brother, two years her junior, was dying to move out of the house. My mother's first husband was an angry man, taking his rage out on her and my siblings. I understand better now, as an adult and social worker, why my brother was always brooding and my sister was anxious.

Education wasn't simply a desire of mine; it was an escape plan. While my family provided me with a foundation that I am grateful for, my home was chaotic and relationships were often dysfunctional. Going to college would provide more opportunities than I would ever have staying at home and getting a job. My parents modeled the importance of a strong work ethic for me, but I wanted more than just a job. I wanted to love what I would be doing for the rest of my life. I would hear them gripe and complain about having to go back to work and I didn't want that for myself. I am grateful that I was aware enough to learn from them what I didn't want just as much as what I did.

My first introduction to social work was in the form of a compassionate and nurturing woman named Laura Orth. I was an angsty and despondent teenager, struggling to figure out who I was amongst the chaos in my home. I landed in Laura's office, a serene environment with inviting artwork and comfy furniture. She was soft-spoken and unassuming. She often sat crisscross applesauce in her big office chair with her hands in her lap. She oozed warmth and care, exactly what I needed at the time but didn't realize.

Laura met so many of my needs in an almost sneaky fashion. It wasn't until years after I started seeing her that I became aware of the power of the therapeutic connection. Her ability to provide unconditional positive regard and the basic acceptance and support of a person regardless of what they say or do made me feel seen and heard during a developmental period in which I was struggling. She never offered advice or criticism, and never told me what to do. But still, there was a magical feeling between us that I could never quite put my finger on, and was one of the reasons I kept seeing her. After I was accepted into graduate school, Laura shared with me that she was an alumna of the same school. It was a beautiful circle that the Universe had been weaving all along.

The path by which I landed in graduate school for social work was not my choosing. I completed my associate degree from a small but influential school in Quincy, Massachusetts. My family is rich in work ethic but limited in financial resources, making going to college not just a challenge but impossible. I chose to attend a two-year college program because I could work and pay by the credit hour, making me very busy but without student loans. When it came time to transfer to a four-year school, I was concerned about the financial impact it would have on me. I heard a professor say, "Any money you spend on education will always be money well spent," and I decided to bite the bullet. Simmons was the perfect fit for me. Tucked away in a part of Boston known as "The Fenway", it was an all-female private institution with historic buildings and small class sizes. I was enrolled as a Dix Scholar because of my age and being a non-traditional commuter student. I loved the organization for the Dix Scholars, and I even ran for a position in the student government. I was starting to gain a feel for what college kids talked about. I continued working full-time as a live-in nanny, commuted to school an hour each way, and did my assignments when the children were napping and on the weekends. I initially majored in nursing at Quincy College, but after my first general education requirement I was hooked on psychology. There was so much to it: human behavior, cognition, medication, mental illness, you name it. While I was devouring every psychology class Simmons offered, my academic advisor was setting up internships so I could figure out what I wanted to be when I grew up. I had been very vocal about my desire to work in research and attend Cornell or Stanford. But since then, I've realized that the best path for me in life tends to come after I make plans that fall apart. In these times, I now figure life is either offering a lesson, or maybe just laughing at me. Either way, I try to pay attention.

The hectic morning of my GRE test became the best thing that ever happened to me. I sideswiped another vehicle trying to make a right hand turn and ripped their side mirror off. This encounter made me late and anxious for the test. Several weeks later when I received my test scores, I hadn't even scored high enough to attend a state school, never mind Stanford. I was distraught. I had put all my eggs in that basket and didn't know what I was going to do. Thank goodness my academic advisor was well-seasoned and always had a backup plan for her students who were as narrow-sighted as I was. She suggested I apply to a couple of social work schools including Simmons. She explained how versatile of a degree it was and rattled off about two dozen types of jobs I could do with a social work education. I was intrigued—but more than that, I was desperate.

I acquired my spot at Smith College School for Social Work in August 2005. I remember walking around the campus, jaw on the ground at how beautiful and fancy it was. I was a poor kid from the South of Boston, first generation college graduate, walking around the grounds of one of the best colleges in the nation. I felt very small and very big all at the same time. Sort of like, "Look at me now!" The program was rigorous. It was a block design, meaning I went to classes for ten weeks to cram in the equivalent of two semesters, then was assigned an internship placement somewhere in the country for nine months. This was where the real learning happened. Between the amount of work, expectations from the school, and my own insecurities, there were times when I thought it wasn't possible. One thing was certain, I gobbled up every sentence of the hundreds of pages of assigned readings a week. I was fascinated by the various diagnoses; intrigued by the treatment modalities; and amazed by the myriad of ways one could practice. And that was just the classroom material. My first internship took me to New Haven, Connecticut where our supervisors gave myself and four other Smithies (as we commonly referred to ourselves) a caseload of underprivileged children to work with. Most of the children I saw during my nine months were from low-income families, usually with a single mother and multiple siblings. These children were wrought with trauma at such young ages. Some had witnessed horrific acts of violence, some were victims of sexual abuse, some had endured both, and many didn't know where their next meal was coming from.

Most kids liked my office. I had toys, games, and coloring books. Sometimes we would "play" with the dolls and the children would re-enact something related to their trauma. I'll be honest; I felt wildly incompetent in what to do with a 5-year-old who laid the "daddy" doll on top of the "mommy" doll. Despite not having a clue which therapeutic intervention I was supposed to use, I would come to realize I was doing more good than harm with my clients. I couldn't tell you whether I was utilizing Freud, Bowlby, or Ainsworth, but I was giving these children my undivided attention, praising them in place of expected criticism, and holding space for their sadness and fear. I would come to learn that those fundamental elements of connection far outweigh my ability to cite a single theoretical orientation.

Another summer of classes passed, and I was off to Los Angeles, California for my final internship. I wasn't sure I was going to like medical social work. The idea of writing discharge plans and working within the bureaucracy of a large establishment didn't appeal to me, but after two months I was hooked. I had the honor of working with children and their families in almost every specialty in the hospital: forensics in the emergency room, cleft palate reconstruction, and hematology/oncology. I started grief groups for parents of infants in the CTICU, helped facilitate palliative care for the family of a two-year-old with Spinal Muscular Atrophy, and learned significant information about how to identify physical abuse on a child in the ER. Although difficult, I am certain that my experiences with terminally ill children and their families molded me into the clinician I am today. Those brave people taught me to embrace grief, honor the process of dying, and meet people exactly where they are. The longer I was in school and the more I learned, I wanted to go back to Simmons and hug my academic advisor. How could she have known this is what I was meant to do?

But outside my professional groove, six months after I moved for work in 2016, I found myself seeking out therapy again. I was in a new place, no friends, and some of my less than desirable behaviors were resurfacing. It took three different therapists to find someone I clicked with. Lee McMichael became a beacon of light for me, just like my first therapist twenty years prior. Lee had a warmth and nurturing vibe to her that you could experience simply by walking past her, no words needed. I saw her for several years as often as she would allow because I craved that connection. I learned about myself, the therapeutic process, and the power of just sitting with someone when they are in pain to be monumental. It came so naturally to her, and I wanted to be that good for my clients. She listened to me without judgment, held space for my pain, and was almost maddeningly consistent. But I had no idea. It wasn't until years later I realized all that she had done for me, all that I had absorbed.

How do I know that I was meant to do this work? I think back to my childhood and the grumblings of adults on Sunday evenings when work is impending. Not only do I never grumble about going to work, I still get excited about it on Sunday evenings. A supervisor told me one time that if being a therapist stops feeling easy like putting on a pair of worn, comfortable jeans, I should look for something else to do. He continued, "What we get to do every day is a privilege. If you stop seeing it that way, you can't be effective." I am in my fifteenth year practicing as a clinical social worker, and I am just starting to feel like I have a clue about what I am doing. I don't think this is because I am a slow learner, but rather that I have embraced the individual nature of each of my experiences. I have been fortunate to be employed in six different social work careers. Each has taught me something new, leaving me with a better understanding of myself, and all of them providing a level of humility I didn't previously have.

I currently work in a holistic private practice with four other amazing therapists and an office manager who saves my bacon regularly! After having lived experiences in medication-assisted treatment, community mental health, and intensive outpatient programs, I have honed my skill set. I specialize in trauma, addiction, and grief, which manifest as three of the most volatile experiences a person can have. I listen to stories of pain, uncertainty, resilience, and hope daily. The people I am privileged to work with have afforded me their trust, something I do not take lightly. I use that trust to show them about themselves, and though a common misconception, I do not tell them what to do. We talk about how to change behavioral patterns that aren't working for them, process traumatic experiences that they may have never talked about before with anyone, and learn ways to feel empowered by the control they discover in therapy that they have over themselves. But most of all, I listen, I see them, I talk without judgment, and I am consistent. Said more simply, I connect with them. Because at the end of the session, they may not remember anything I have said, but I guarantee they will remember how they felt.

I will never discount the amazing formal education I received—never —but I must qualify it. Education gives us a solid foundation, and it is from this foundation which we build our careers. Everyone builds differently, which is why some therapists are better suited for certain clients.

Every continuing education class we take, conference we attend, client we see, colleague we connect with, and hour we spend in our own therapy enhances what school gave us. Both of my most influential experiences with social workers have been based in connection. Each did it beautifully, so well that I didn't even know it was happening at the time. Both of these women helped to shape me into the therapist I am today, emotionally, and professionally. Now I try to do the same for others, one hour at a time.

Pearl of Wisdom
"Feeling attached to another human being feeds the soul. The soul heals through connection with others, and through it we can begin to grow, thrive, and give back."
~ Nicole Young

ABOUT THE AUTHOR

Nicole Young is the co-founder and COO of Journey Through Counseling, LLC, a holistic based private practice in Bowling Green, KY. She empowers people to own their stories through the emotional restoration of connection within the therapeutic relationship. She specializes in helping people heal from complex trauma, addiction, and grief. Nicole recently presented at the International Brainspotting Conference on the topic of complex trauma and resiliency. Her passion for this work stems from witnessing people rebuild their lives in the face of extraordinary circumstances. When she isn't working, Nicole enjoys CrossFit, snuggling with her Westie, Dexter, and spending time with her powerful tribe of women.

Website: www.journeythroughcounseling.com
Instagram: journey_through_counseling
Facebook: @journeythroughcounseling
Email: Nicole@jtcwc.com

15

CHRISTINA BRODERICK, MSW, LSW

TRANSFORMING OUR EXPERIENCES

I AM the daughter of a Jamaican mother born second in her family of nine and the first to immigrate to the United States. Raised solely by her—with heavy support from my grandmother—I am the youngest of three children, a Jersey-bred, first-generation American, first-generation college graduate, and first-generation business owner.

Before diving into the successful company I have created, it's important to understand the journey.

After much mental and emotional turmoil, my father left when I was two-years-old to return back to Jamaica. Unwilling to pay child support, he left my mother with one income to now support us all. While we would spend most of our summers going to Jamaica to be with family, (including a short stint in summer school,) the hardship caught up to us a few years later as we lost the house due to foreclosure. To avoid going to a shelter, we temporarily moved into her friend's basement for housing.

Now, this wasn't a luxurious basement with designated rooms and spaces for us to spread out. This was four people, three of which were all under 10-years-old, in one room using household items to "create" bedrooms. Until this day, that experience is still one of the most pivotal moments of my life that I can remember—not just because of how difficult it was financially, but mentally and emotionally, realizing at any moment external circumstances can completely change all that you have come to know.

One weekend morning, I distinctly remember laying in my makeshift bedroom wanting to sleep the entire day away; to live in my dreams and not face my current reality…and believe me, I tried very hard! But of course, I was left with no other option than to handle the truth. It was this moment, coupled with continued similar experiences, that my need today for expansiveness, space and security was originally rooted.

Despite our financial hardships, education was always a top priority. We went to Catholic schools in neighboring towns, as ours did not have a quality education system. While my mother didn't always pay on time and there were threats of disenrollment due to missed payments, if there's one thing to know about my mom, it's that she will always find a way to make sure her children are taken care of. So yes, while we lived in a basement, we would come running out in our uniforms from the back of the house where the basement door was located to catch the bus to the next town for school.

However, this decision was not without scrutiny from others. People could not understand why my mother couldn't afford a home yet was paying thousands of dollars to send her kids to school. She worked hard to afford what she could, when she could, leaving for work some days before we would wake up and coming home after we had gone to sleep. Yet, as the phrase goes, "Mothers always know best," and I know I can credit much of my success today to the many tough decisions she had to make for our education.

To distract me from the hardships we faced, from a young age, I always had a jam-packed schedule. I played multiple sports during the same season and would spend many days, nights and weekends with friends. Of course, my friends and their families had their own problems, but everything just seemed so much better than my circumstances. It was nice to immerse myself into someone else's life filled with things I didn't have, like pets, two parents, pools and vacations.

Their families and lives just seemed much simpler and as time went on, I began to become more curious about what certain experiences shape people's lives and the way they operate in the world. For example, while my sister and I did well in school, stayed out of trouble and maintained healthy social lives, my brother struggled in all of those areas growing up. I just didn't get why life seemed to be so much harder for him.

Therefore, as I graduated high school and began college, I knew a psychology major made the most sense to pursue this interest. However, during my first year at La Salle University, I realized that I wanted to attach myself to something greater and to be challenged in a different way. While maintaining my psychology major, I decided to add on a Spanish minor and began taking pre-med classes to become a doctor. As I recognized that the road to becoming a doctor was long, arduous and expensive, the prestige and assumedly lucrative career was enticing enough for me to go all-in with the hopes to make my immigrant mother proud and the opportunity to provide for her and the family.

While managing multiple on-campus jobs, extracurricular activities, leadership positions, my heavy course load and an overly thriving social life (college, right?), I was fortunate enough to study abroad on the island of Mallorca one summer to finish off my Spanish minor. During midday trips to the most beautiful beaches and exploring a new culture, I began to really expand the future I envisioned for myself for the first time; a future where I could actively explore the world and not be confined to limited options and only what's familiar. This realization would later drive my future in entrepreneurship.

If there's one thing about me, it's that I take action—and fast. So, after returning back to school for the fall semester of my senior year, I decided to take a gap year after graduation to better position myself for medical school. In my new desire to expand my experiences, I joined a year-long AmeriCorps program in Los Angeles, California called City Year. I had never been so excited to move somewhere where I didn't know one single person and take on actual responsibilities like rent and bills, but even the chance to no longer deal with snowy winters was all I needed.

Turns out, while I thought I was just getting warmer weather, I in-turn received an experience that ended up completely changing the trajectory of my entire life.

While I was in California, I was still applying for medical school yet could only afford a handful of applications. Luckily enough, I received invitations to interview at different schools. However, each time I showed up, I would pray that they didn't ask, "Why do you want to be a doctor?" because I knew deep down that I didn't have a strong answer.

The truth is, I was doing it because it was a healthy challenge mixed with the prestige of wanting to be a doctor, but I knew that long-term it wasn't what I wanted to do. This really hit home for me when I was in a casual conversation with a physician, and he asked me directly, "Could you see yourself doing something else with your life and being equally as happy?" Without pause, I responded, "Yes!" and he told me to do that instead.

It wasn't until then that I recognized the need I had for the external affirmation that I could still change the direction of my life—that it was *okay* to make a shift. To have spent many years and thousands of dollars on one thing to then drop it all was very scary…yet freeing. Fortunately for me, it also helped that I was waitlisted to the medical schools I interviewed for and then ultimately was not accepted.

When my Corps year ended and having changed directions, I had to figure out what was next for my path. I knew I really enjoyed the experience I just had working in an elementary school in Watts, and I loved being able to have an impact on the youth but knew that the traditional educator path wasn't the direction that felt right for me.

After a fun and liberating year in Los Angeles, I moved back to New Jersey and began to work in a Neuroscience & Neuropsychology lab as a research assistant on studies for people with multiple sclerosis and traumatic brain injuries. While working there, I thought maybe I could get my PhD in research and tie into my degree in psychology; however, the more time I spent there, the more I realized that research also was not the space for me.

Left confused about the future, I began to reflect on my experience in California and wanted to return in some way to the education space. Education was so pivotal in my life and I knew that it was the space I wanted to leave my mark.

In my search for what was next, I stumbled upon social work.

Like most of society, I had the preconceived notion that social work involved working for the state and within child welfare. I was oblivious to the depth and expansiveness the field truly possesses. Upon learning about the vastness the field presents, I began to look at different social work programs for my Master's Degree and ultimately landed on Boston University's online program. Their curriculum stood out to me more than the others and the flow of the program allowed me to continue to work my jobs to pay for rent, student loans and all of the other adulting responsibilities.

Throughout my Master's program, I made sure that I took the *intentional* time to intern at places that brought me closer to connecting with students. My first internship was in a transitional residence for kids ages five through twelve who no longer needed inpatient psychiatric help but weren't stable enough to return back home. They stayed at the residence for six to eight months to receive therapeutic support and alternative schooling. While I learned *a lot*, especially through witnessing the traumas such young children experienced at the hands of the adults responsible for their care, I recognized that this was also not the space for me. The traumas were too heavy and the environment was difficult.

Now, I must note that when starting my Master's program, I knew I didn't want to be a therapist. Instead I wanted to run a business, but thought it would be a non-profit organization for the community because that's what social workers did: worked in non-profits! So, while I enrolled in a clinical program, my goal was to first learn how to best support clients on an individual level to be able to then best serve on a larger scale.

I went on to intern at a high school where I was able to get a taste of what macro social work entailed. I was tasked with running an after-school program, running their conflict resolution program and writing a state-funded grant that I was then awarded $10,000 for to create and implement my Anti-Poverty Civic & Engagement Fellowship for the high school students. This experience taught me a lot about how schools operate from a different perspective than the one I had in California.

Employment-wise, during this time I began to work for a federally funded program called Early Intervention where I served as a regional coordinator for families with babies from birth to three-years-old with special needs or disabilities. The role included going out into the community to educate about the services and training any new statewide staff to the program.

Once I finished my Master's program and passed my licensing exam, I was fortunate to have a program coordinator job lined up at Rutgers University. Student Support Services is a federally funded TRIO program that supports first-generation, low-income college students. Due to my own background, working with this population felt so familiar.

It was during this time that I was approached by a colleague turned good friend, Shy Yi, who gave me the idea that I should start my own business. She told me that students really resonated with me, that I have a great presence and, among other things, all that would lend itself to me being a successful entrepreneur. While at first I turned down the idea, it resurfaced my prior thoughts about wanting to run a nonprofit, as well as how all my personal and professional experiences can be used to serve others more strategically.

More specifically, in my reflection, time and time again I witnessed students struggling with their mental health but not knowing what to do or even that it was a problem. I would watch overly stressed students run away from me to throw up in trash cans, or about to pass out from not eating all day, or would tell me that despite the serious challenges going on at home, they were black and "black people don't go to therapy," and subsequently finding themselves breaking down in the middle of a 300 person lecture. Or the students who had so much pressure on them because they were the first in their family to go to college that they began to drink and developed an alcohol disorder. Overwhelmingly, I witnessed students who overall developed unhealthy coping skills as they were just trying to get good grades, graduate and make their family proud, a situation I knew all too well.

It was time to make a change in how we approach student mental health. In January 2018, I launched the initial version of my company, Student Success Coaching, where I was going to coach students and parents on mental health and wellness tips.

As I began to learn more about the difficulties of working in higher education, business and the direction I wanted my company to go, I took a new job as a school social worker in a middle school. While there, I noticed the gap in mental health literacy was even more prominent, having picked up children off of bathroom floors who were having panic attacks because of all of the stress that they had going on in their lives, and who didn't know how to handle it at thirteen.

The education system has put more and more pressure on students to perform well academically; however, I was witnessing first-hand that when we put their mental health on the backburner, it's infinitely harder for them to reach their academic and life goals.

I knew that there was a different way for students to learn how they can tackle their mental health along their educational journey. Combining my expertise within mental health as well as my history throughout the system from K12 through higher education, I was able to evolve my company into what it is today.

Our mission is to transform the way that we as a society approach mental health. In June 2020, seeking freedom, flexibility and expansion, I was fortunate enough to go full-time in my business, while at the time, continuing part-time as a psychotherapist until January 2021, and an Adjunct Professor for up and coming social workers.

While initially, my company solely focused on the education space with schools, districts and education programs nationwide, we've also begun working with corporate clients on ways that their employees can begin to take charge of their mental health journey.

Upon leaping full-time into my business in June of 2020 during a global pandemic, my company grew substantially, accumulating almost $100,000 in revenue in eighteen months and serving thousands of students, families and organizations nationwide through our mental health programming and consulting initiatives.

Most recently, I've felt a calling to expand the ways I can serve, particularly within the field of social work. Typically, as social workers, our scopes are limited in regards to the work we think we can do: the standard spaces of schools, child welfare, medical, policy, nonprofits, etc. However, as a profession that requires us to be highly skilled and trained, the possibilities for our impact are more boundless than we realize.

As such, I've begun to coach and consult for other social workers who are looking to build and grow a service-based business. With the upcoming launch of the Social Work Entrepreneurship Incubator and as a soon-to-be certified small business consultant, I want social workers to learn how they can use entrepreneurship to fulfill their life dreams.

In closing, it's important to recognize that we don't have to be placed in a box, limited to our past, education, geographic location, etc. We don't have to limit our abilities to what people say that we can do or how much we can earn. We have more control than we think we do, and once we can really harness that power, we become a force unlike any other.

It is my mission in life for society to change the way that we approach mental health, and help people recognize the opportunities that are available to them so they can take charge of the directions of their lives.

Currently, I am the owner of a mental health consulting company, adjunct professor, and business consultant to social workers; I'm a mixture of being in social work, around social work and out of social work. It has been truly exhilarating yet mind-blowing to see how my degree and my experience have both allowed me to open the possibilities for all of the ways that I can maximize my impact on the world.

My future is brighter than I could have ever dreamed, reflecting back to when I was laying in that basement hoping for better days. I desire to give back to my mother for her continued sacrifices for the family, cherish my relationships with my close friends and soon-to-be husband, and, overall, lean into slowing down, embracing all that life has to offer, and expand beyond belief.

My final thought for you and pearl of wisdom comes from one of my favorite quotes.

Pearl of Wisdom

"You cannot control everything that happens to you in life, but you can fundamentally transform your experience.
Life happens, our lived experiences are valid, and with that we still have the ability to take charge over the direction of our lives."
~ Christina Broderick

ABOUT THE AUTHOR

Christina Broderick is a Licensed Social Worker, a former Psychotherapist, a Certified School Social Worker, an Adjunct Professor, and a business owner, who is passionate about ensuring people live in their purpose and mental health becomes a priority for all.

Having worked across the entire lifespan, Christina founded Broderick and Company Consulting (formerly IgnitEDU) in 2018, a premier agency with the aim to provide mental health education, training, and resources to K12/higher education programs and corporations looking to strengthen the supports and practices of their community, as well as business coaching for social workers building service-based, impact-driven businesses.

As a first-generation American and college graduate, Christina holds a Bachelor's Degree in Psychology, with a minor in Spanish from La Salle University in Philadelphia and a Master's Degree in Social Work from Boston University.

Website: www.broderickandco.com

16

JIHAN ALI, MSW, LICSW

A JOURNEY DEVELOPED THROUGH MANY MOMENTS

I WAS BORN IN MOGADISHU, Somalia, and at the age of six years old, one of the most bloody and violent conflicts in the region's history broke out. What was once an idyllic childhood was completely turned upside down when the Somali civil war erupted. Instead of watching Saturday morning cartoons, my childhood consisted of moving between safe houses and refugee camps, all while avoiding armed soldiers with a vendetta to find and execute families that were in any way affiliated with the previous government of Somalia or of a tribe different from them. This put a very real and dangerous target on families such as my own. At an age when most children were learning to read and play sports, I had seen and experienced firsthand what the atrocities of war and poverty can do to social welfare. It was difficult to find safety since customary law had collapsed due to the fighting. Even when the fighting ceased, there were still armed militia roaming streets, and depending on what your tribe was, you still didn't want to find yourself in the "wrong" neighborhood. As a young girl, there didn't appear to be many prospects; structures and schools had collapsed. My parents valued education and partnered with another family in the neighborhood to hire a trained teacher. They gave him whatever they could find for him to teach me, my two sisters and the neighboring girl math, English, and Quran for two hours a day across four to five days a week.

With the help of extended family members, my family was able to get out of Somalia and into Kenya. We lived in a refugee camp in Kenya. In 1996, my family and I entered the United States as refugees. The refugee camp felt like a separate country from the rest of the town as everyone there was of Somali descent, but stepping out of the camp was a totally different world with different language and customs. At the time, my mom had seven children and was pregnant with an eighth. I was responsible to help with my younger siblings as well as run to the market daily for perishable items needed to make our food as we did not have a refrigerator. We did not go to school at this time but my mom ensured that we did not lose what we had learned by spending some time with us to go over different lesson plans.

I was twelve years old when we entered the United States and was placed in the seventh grade based on my age. I had a limited education and spoke very little English, but I was determined to make the most of this new opportunity. I remember sitting in classes like social studies and science and not understanding what the teacher was explaining to us, let alone knowing how to complete the homework assignments. I remember an assignment in communication class where I had to give a speech in front of the class and be videotaped while giving the speech. I can't tell you what my topic was or what I said, but I remember that assignment vividly because of the fear it brought me. Now it makes me smile to think about it. How unrealistic it was to expect a seventh grader who had a few months of schooling and spoke very little English to give a speech in class and be recorded. I don't remember if the rest of the class watched. I don't know how I passed any of my classes but I am sure the teachers knew what they were doing. Math was my favorite subject as it didn't require a lot of words. I dreaded writing class, but learned that every paper should have an introduction, body and conclusion which came in handy during those twenty-to-thirty-page papers in graduate school. In eighth grade, I found myself under-standing my teachers more. I can't really tell you when I began to completely grasp words and concepts that were so foreign to me not so long before. I worked hard to overcome every obstacle I encountered.

While in high school, I thought often about what professions were possible aside from being a doctor, lawyer, engineer or a teacher. I really enjoyed my sociology and psychology classes in high school and knew I wanted a job that allowed me to work with others and help those who needed support. Being from an immigrant family, social work was not a profession I was familiar with. I did not have very much guidance from school counselors on the different options that were available to me for schools I could attend and majors I could choose. Maybe they thought my parents would help steer me in the right direction. I was the first person in my family to go to college. Even though we had only recently adjusted from life as refugees, as the eldest of eleven children, it wasn't an option that I earn a college degree but an expectation. My parents often said, "The rest will follow in your footsteps," whether good or bad, which at times put a lot of pressure on me to be perfect. My father told all of his children that higher education would afford us options in life and supported us in achieving it. My mom used to joke that we could get my father to do whatever we wanted as long as we said it was for school. He would show up to school unexpectedly to make sure we were in our classes and attended every parent-teacher conference, but would allow us to translate for him which helped us fudge the truth when we needed to! Being the first person in my family to go to college presented its challenges as I lacked guidance. After graduating from high school, I knew that I had to further my education and decided that I wanted to choose a major that allowed me to help others. While attending community college, I became interested in criminal justice as a way to help others. I dreamed of one day being able to help individuals and families in hopes of emulating the kindness and compassion that people had offered to me and my family when we were escaping the Somali civil war.

To make this dream possible, I was able to figure out I needed to attend a university and gain a bachelor's degree; this meant I needed to make sure all of the credits I completed in community college would transfer and find a college that offered a bachelor's degree in criminal justice. I chose to complete an Associate of Arts degree in community college to ensure all of my credits transferred and found a Bachelors in Criminal Justice program at Metropolitan state university. I took classes with people who wanted to work as police officers, in corrections, and nurses, and was taught by instructors who already worked in the criminal justice field as lieutenants, captains and sergeants of police departments. This allowed me to broaden my perspective as well as expose me to many viewpoints. Some of their opinions surprised me which made me want to be a part of this field more, if only to offer a different perspective. I wanted to bring a broader lens and challenge certain viewpoints, and found the opportunities to start through the topics I picked for my presentations and the questions I asked when others offered a narrow viewpoint.

After graduating with my bachelor's degree, I found three part time jobs. One of my jobs was as a youth worker at a juvenile correctional facility, the second was as a youth worker at a group home and the third, a case manager at a nonprofit organization working with truant high school students. While working these jobs, I discovered that I wanted to work with individuals *before* they were at risk of entering or already in correctional facilities. I wanted to work with individuals while they were still in their communities. I wanted to help individuals work through whatever it was that was contributing to truancy and criminal behaviors in an effort to understand and address behavioral issues. I realized that most of the youth returned to the same neighbor-hoods that would continue to offer the same conditions that led them to be in the situation they were currently in, and felt I couldn't offer different options or perspectives in what I was doing in my current positions. Not long after beginning my new jobs, I heard about social work and began inquiring to people, reading material, and deciding social work was the right path for me. That same year, I was accepted into a Masters of Social Work (MSW) program and was excited to begin my new endeavor.

Since I was ten years old, I knew that I wanted to work with and help others. I knew I wanted to be like the aid workers that helped my family and countless others in the refugee camps. At that time, I did not have the language to define what they did or the job titles they held, but I knew I wanted to do the type of work they did. Graduate school at last allowed me to accomplish that goal.

While in graduate school, I learned about different theories and tech-niques. I learned that individuals have strengths and resources and that my role as a social worker would be to help build upon those skills and resources. I learned about social justice and advocacy. I also learned about attachment theory and became extremely interested. To me, attachment theory explained patterns that are created by trauma and unhealthy relationships. It explains why people engage in behaviors that can be deemed inappropriate or even criminal. I completed two internships while in graduate school: one allowed me to work with low-income communities to learn about and pursue homeownership, and the other allowed me to work in mental health with individuals and families as a skills trainer and an in-home therapist. Completing these internships made me realize that I had made the right decision in pursuing a social work degree.

After graduation, I took a job that allowed me to work with adults and children in their home. I provided both individual and family skills training and therapy and did group work with adults and children. This allowed me to hone my clinical skills, explore what I wanted to do with my social work degree, and pursue a clinical license. I took my LGSW test and started the process of working towards my LICSW. But let me tell you something: while working as an in-home skills trainer and therapist with adults and adolescence, I learned what self-determination really looked like in practice and not just in theory. I was so excited to help people and wanted to do whatever I could to help support the individuals I worked with meet their goals. I soon found myself experiencing compassion fatigue and had to learn the true meaning of self-determination myself. I had to come to terms with the very fact that just because I saw the steps needed to achieve a goal, it did not mean that the person I was working with was ready to take those steps, and I had to be ok with that. The hardest part was understanding and accepting the pace that the individual wanted to go at, even if it meant no movement. Along with self-determination, I learned the true meaning of words like autonomy and boundaries. This helped with my longevity in the field and continue to be words that I share with incoming social workers.

While working on my clinical license, I got an opportunity to join a two-year certificate program called Trauma Focused Cognitive Behavioral Therapy. The program allowed me to obtain the tools needed to become a qualified therapist and begin working with individuals who had experienced severe trauma. I continued to work as a Mental Health Practitioner providing in home skills and therapy to adolescents, adults and children while completing the two-year program. The program emphasized helping children and adolescence work through traumatic experiences.

While working on my clinical license, I wanted to continue to increase my knowledge base and began working part time at an adult foster care. This opportunity allowed me to gain more experience with the adult population who were struggling with severe and persistent mental illness (SPMI). I really enjoyed this work as it allowed me to partner with individuals in setting goals around gaining more independence and offering support and guidance to meet those goals.

Social work also led me to work as a Senior Psychiatric Social Worker in Hennepin County, the largest and most diverse county in Minnesota. My work was with the crisis program as a crisis responder and stabilization provider. I worked with individuals having a crisis in the community to help provide support and resources including clients who struggled with mental or chemical health issues and access to the resources necessary to stabilize their health. This role also allowed me to work with individuals who were at risk to themselves or others but were not ready to engage in services. I completed assessments which allowed me to recommend the appropriate intervention, and we worked very hard to ensure we were able to keep and support individuals in their homes by offering resources to help stabilize the crisis and help limit or remove barriers to services. As a mental health professional, I often offered consultation to newer staff or those still working on their licensure. It was these experiences that helped me realize that I really enjoyed training and teaching. I took supervision classes at the University of Minnesota and started to offer clinical supervision as well as pursue leadership opportunities.

In 2017, I had an opportunity to join a six-month certificate program with Harvard Medical School and received a certificate in Global Mental Health: Trauma and Recovery. This program offered a global perspective and focused on refugee trauma, which allowed me to increase my knowledge base as it related to trauma and trauma-informed intervention. The program included two-week in-person lectures led by instructors who worked with refugees in various fields, and the rest of the time was virtual. I was able to meet social workers, psychologists, medical doctors, psychiatrists, professors, human rights advocates, and many more professionals from all over the world who worked with refugees and asylees. It was an invaluable experience.

Since 2020, I have been working as an Early Childhood Mental Health Consultant where I have had even more opportunities to learn and explore what else the profession of social work has to offer. It has allowed me to stretch my brain and imagine what else I can do as a social worker. It has also allowed me to practice and improve my reflective supervision skills and work with some great people who have been in the field of early childhood mental health for many years, and who I am so lucky to learn from.

As I reflect on social work, I often think about how to introduce social work to communities that often see social workers as only "those people that take your kids away". I also think about how to introduce us social workers to those communities. What I mean is how we as social workers can think more creatively about how to apply the concepts we have learned in school, books, and articles to diverse communities who were not thought about when these concepts were originally developed. When I work with communities where mental health diagnoses are foreign, including my community, I often talk about symptoms instead of throwing about diagnoses because, at the end of the day, we are taught to meet the individual where they are. I believe social work has the ability to meet *everyone* where they are at and not only those who were thought about when the concepts and theories were developed. Social work at its conception looked very different from the clinical work some of us do now.

While doing this work, I have found that the majority of the individuals I come across have experienced trauma or complex trauma. Many experienced trauma as children and some continue to experience it into adulthood. Several of the individuals I meet are immigrants or refugees and have experienced war and famine. Some have witnessed family members being killed or have themselves been at risk of losing their lives. Some have sustained physical injuries, but all have sustained emotional injuries that continue to affect them in their daily lives.

I knew in my heart that I wanted to work with others from a very young age, and social work has allowed me the opportunity to see it through. I have been on a journey with social work for some years now, and I plan on continuing to learn and see where this journey will take me. I have had the opportunity to engage in a wide variety of opportunities and have met some great people. I hope to continue stretching my imagination and exploring where else my relationship with social work will lead me.

Pearl of Wisdom

"Social work is for all of us. I believe social work has the ability to meet everyone where they are at and not only those who were thought about when certain concepts and theories were developed."

~Jihan Ali

ABOUT THE AUTHOR

Jihan Ali, MSW, LICSW has been in the field of social work for over 10 years and in various capacities. Her experience includes direct services in the areas of crisis and stabilization work, psychotherapy to children and adults as well as work in the criminal justice system. Jihan has experience as a supervisor and in program management. She provides clinical supervision to up and coming clinicians and enjoys teaching and training. Jihan provides Early Childhood mental health consultation and reflective supervision to early childhood providers. Jihan has been trained in TF-CBT, Motivational interviewing and has completed a Global Mental Health: Trauma and Recovery certificate through Harvard Medical School, Department of Continuing Education. Over the past 10 years, she has provided outreach to underserved communities around mental health resources. Jihan has provided trainings in the areas of culturally responsive services, suicidality and safety planning. Jihan is originally from Somalia and has called Minnesota home since 1996.

17

JEREMY CARNEY, MSW, PH.D.

SOCIAL WORK EDUCATION AND PRACTICE: A FULL CIRCLE JOURNEY

RAY DIDN'T WANT to go to school. He only had a few friends and didn't like his teachers. He refused to go, and his single-parent mother had given up on fighting with him about it. After missing a lot of the first part of sixth grade, a referral was made to social services and a case worker was assigned. After spending some time with Ray to develop a relationship and assess the situation, it turns out he hated the bus ride to school in the morning and home in the afternoon. Some of the older children were picking on him and he didn't think the bus driver or teachers cared.

"How about if I gave you a ride to school? It's on my way to work," I asked.

"I suppose," said Ray.

For the next six months, I gave Ray a ride to school most days. On the way to school, we'd talk about all kinds of things that were part of an eleven-year old's life. Things like video games and TV shows. We'd also talk about ways to make school work. It wouldn't be true to say this was a perfect helping relationship. Somedays Ray didn't want to talk and, on a few occasions, he would still refuse to go to school. At the end of the school year, Ray participated in a group canoe trip we put together. He'd never been camping before and seemed to really enjoy the experience. Sitting around that campfire on our last evening, he said,

"Thanks for all the stuff with school and all, but I don't think I need that anymore." Ray did go on to graduate and did indeed not need any more help from a social worker to get to school.

When people ask me what's rewarding about being a social worker, it's people like Ray that come to mind. For almost thirty years, I've been a social worker, with the majority of that time spent in higher education. Over time, I've had the privilege of developing relationships with thousands of people, some based on helping and some on learning. Not all went as well as it did with Ray. Some of those helping relationships didn't have a positive outcome that I was able to see. Some of the systems I found myself working with seemed ineffective and unyielding. I've been frustrated and at times angry. I've also helped people navigate some challenging situations often by just listening and ensuring that they know I care.

What led me to a career in social work? The answer for me, like most people I suspect, is complicated. Looking back, the foundation was built through my upbringing and family experiences. My folks were very progressive in their personal and political views. It wasn't uncommon for them to host our rural countryside democratic caucus at our home. They didn't necessarily use terms like "social justice" or "dignity and worth of all people," but these were ideas that were important to them and made clear to me and my siblings. We had our struggles as a family as well. When I was very young, we were impoverished. My parents took advantage of some of the social programs available to help us improve our lives. For example, I went to Headstart as a child for the benefits of early childhood education. Another defining experience for me was becoming a father at age twenty-two. Jennifer and I, like many young parents, were scared and felt ill-prepared to take on the responsibility of a family. We received support from public and private agencies that helped us survive and encouraged us to continue our educational goals.

Despite these experiences, when I went to university, I really didn't know what a social worker was. I knew I wanted a career centered on helping people, but wasn't sure what the best avenue to pursue that would be. I started out as an education major and thought that becoming a teacher would fulfill my goal. But during the first semester, I became disenchanted with the idea of working in a rigidly structured school system. I wandered around campus and visited different depart-

166

ments to explore majors; late in the day, I came across the Department of Social Work. There was a professor who happened to have some office time available and agreed to meet with me. An hour later, I changed my major to social work.

What was it that convinced me that this was the education I was looking for? The values of the profession. That professor explained to me that social work can be thought of as a profession made up of three primary aspects. First, it is a set of *theories* that are used to structure our interventions with different systems. My education to this point had been dominated by theory, and although many were interesting, this facet of social work didn't immediately excite me. Second, social work is a set of *skills* to be used when helping others. The professor told me that I could expect "hands-on" practice experiences as part of my training to learn and hone these skills. Now, this piqued my interest as I was hungry for learning beyond a lecture-based classroom. Finally, she explained social work has an established set of professional *values and ethics* that guide the profession. She gave me a copy of the preamble to the National Association of Social Work Code of Ethics which contains a listing and explanation of the profession's core values. This is what sealed the deal for me that afternoon. I read them and said to myself, "These are some of my most important beliefs as well." It was finding that the profession's established values aligned with my personal values that convinced me to be a social worker.

My first professional job upon graduation was in child protection. Although I had a good education as a generalist social worker, I quickly realized that I faced a steep learning curve in professional child welfare practice. I needed to understand the interpretation of state statutes, learn county social service process and procedures, and develop skills in working with folks who were mostly non-voluntary clients and who had an understandable distrust of the system. It was challenging but very rewarding work. I dealt with many difficult and emotionally taxing situations, but ultimately, I was able to help many children and families remain intact and safe.

I also developed a frustration with the system and a desire to improve it. At the time, state law allowed school officials to file a petition with the court alleging educational neglect after a child had accrued seven unexcused absences. This was happening regularly in our county and set up a situation where our first contact with the family was at the courthouse on the day of the hearing. Needless to say, this was a less than ideal process. The system immediately set up an adversarial situation between the social worker and family, added to an already overburdened court schedule, and facilitated very little communication between the school district and social services. After working with a number of these cases, I found myself getting frustrated and thinking that there has to be a better way to help these children get to school. I put together a plan that would have the elementary school principals make a referral to social services once a child had five unexcused absences. We would in turn conduct a home visit to help problem-solve the situation with the family and in some cases offer voluntary services. My supervisor approved the plan, but was skeptical about its prospects. At that time, there was a rather cool relationship between the school system and social services without a great deal of trust and mutual support. I made an appointment to meet with each elementary school principal in an effort to convince them that my plan was worth trying. They all agreed to give it a try and most were supportive of the idea. The plan worked. We drastically reduced the number of educational neglect hearings in the county and most of the families that we were able to contact developed a strategy to get their children to school consistently. The program became a permanent aspect of our county's child welfare programming. It was a minor victory, but in a profession where challenging or changing established systems often seems incredibly difficult if not impossible, you have to take the small victories when they happen.

It was also at this time of my life and early career when I learned the importance of self-care. Like many social workers, I found myself working with people who were experiencing very difficult circumstances; these were the kinds of situations that most of society likes to pretend don't exist. This type of work will take its toll on you if you don't develop strategies to take care of yourself. I had a colleague whose strategy for self-care was coaching youth sports. I was intrigued as I had always enjoyed sports, but didn't think I could commit to a full coaching schedule. He asked if I'd consider officiating as there was a shortage of referees and didn't require an obligation to a practice schedule. I had done some recreational softball umpiring in college for extra money, but hadn't thought about pursuing anything beyond that. I started officiating high school football, and in short order added basketball and baseball. Many people asked me why in the world I would want to pursue this type of advocation with the crowd yelling criticism at every decision an official makes. My answer at the time was simple: it allowed me to be around kids having fun playing a sport where I knew nothing about their homelife and family struggles. It is a "normalizing" activity for me and allows me to have a very different relationship with people outside of my professional social worker persona. I have found that officiating athletic competitions are some of the most high-pressure and intense experiences I have ever had. In those situations, you have only your partner referees to rely on, and that requires a great deal of trust. My fellow officials have become some of my best friends, confidants, and a wonderful support network.

After a couple of years in child welfare, I applied to graduate school, was accepted, and received financial support through the federal Title IV-E Child Welfare Program. Getting a Master's of Social Work degree provided me with advanced practice knowledge and skills, and also helped to open many career doors for me. Over the course of the next five years, I moved into doing work with runaway and homeless youth and their families. It was my first "clinical" type job providing therapy to individuals and families. This was very rewarding work and my first experience working with a private nonprofit organization. We survived on grants; every year, we would barely make ends meet, but we were able to be creative in the services we provided, unbound by many of the regulations that existed in a governmental agency. Eventually, I decided to take a supervisory position at a psychiatric hospital. At this time, I was quite happy with my new leadership role, but quickly became very disillusioned working in the for-profit mental health world. I saw first-hand how our healthcare system is structured to help those with the best insurance, and how those without are pushed to the margins.

Then, I received a call that would change the trajectory of my career. A former professor contacted me to determine if I had any interest in teaching a class as an adjunct professor. This caught me quite off-guard as I hadn't envisioned myself teaching. I accepted the offer to teach a child welfare elective class to undergraduates and thoroughly enjoyed the experience. For the next couple of years, I would teach a class when needed and I started to consider a career shift into academia. As serendipity would have it, I learned that the community college in our region had an opening for a full-time instructor in a Mental Health Care Associate program. This two-year degree program was designed to train direct service staff for an antiquated state hospital system. They were looking for someone to transform it into a pre-social work curriculum and develop articulation agreements with regional universities. I was offered the position and excitedly accepted. I would spend the next six years at this institution which helped me prepare for a move to a university professorship in two significant ways. First, I learned how to teach. Shortly after starting as a full-time educator, I realized that as I had no formal training in teaching, I simply taught as I liked to learn as a student. Being able to adapt to different learning styles and student needs was a skill I needed to develop. There were no research expectations of professors and few committee assignments. The professional development opportunities were for the most part centered on teaching and learning, and I tried to learn as much as I could about the science and art of teaching.

The second substantial development was enrolling in a doctorial program. The state system allowed me to use a certain number of tuition waivers to take classes within the system each semester which was a great incentive to further my education. I would take one or two classes in the evenings. Though it made for slow progress, it allowed me to work full-time and still contribute to my family. By this time, Jennifer and I had two small children which definitely added to the challenge of balancing responsibilities. There seems to be a bit of mystique that surrounds earning a doctor of philosophy degree as though you're being granted membership into a certain intellectual club. Although there certainly were scholarly expectations, I found the program to be primarily an exercise in perseverance. Without the encouragement of my family and the financial support of my employer, I'm not sure I would have been able to do it. I started out in a cohort of twenty-four people, of which about half would graduate. Most would finish the course work, but it was the comprehensive exams and dissertation that proved insurmountable. Of the candidates who didn't finish their degree, it wasn't that they couldn't hack the rigors of the program; it was that life got in the way. Once we finished the required classes, the dissertation research, writing, and defense are all independent work. It's an enormous individual project that can easily get derailed. While working on my dissertation, I was made aware of an open faculty position at a local university in their school of social work. I was offered and accepted the appointment, but written into my contract was the stipulation that I needed to have a terminal degree completed by the time my probationary period was over for a tenure decision to be made. Needless to say, this provided a great deal of motivation to successfully complete a dissertation and defend it.

My dissertation explores social work education and ethical relationships. Around the time when I was considering topics, I learned that roughly half of all substantiated ethics violations by social workers had to do with the development of an unethical relationship with a client. This caused me to question how well we were preparing students for the challenges of practice. I had a colleague who once told me that her dissertation became one of the most important aspects of her professional persona. I told her that although my dissertation was by far the largest piece of scholarship I had ever embarked on, I wasn't going to let it define me. She was mostly right and I was mostly wrong. Beyond the publication of my dissertation and a subsequent article, I soon realized that there was a great need for professional development on ethical practice, and my research provided ample content for continuing education for practicing social workers. In the past fifteen years, I have presented this material at over fifty local, state, regional, and international conferences and workshops. This work is one of the defining aspects of my career to date and I'm grateful for the opportunities it has offered me.

Today, I continue to train students who want to enter the profession of social work. I love the magic of classroom discussions and the growth that students experience while in our program. I proudly share the theories, skills, and values that are part of this great profession. I also love to travel and explore other cultures. As a professor, I've been able to develop study abroad programs for social work students and have traveled with them to over twelve different countries around the world. Although my full-time job is in academia, I've always kept ties to the realm of social work practice. I've gratefully served on the board of directors of a number of local human service agencies, but it continues to be direct work with clients that grounds me. Students have often remarked that they appreciate the stories I share from my experiences to illustrate theory and its application. Whether it be working in a local shelter or facilitating a group, I've always felt it was important to "keep a foot" in the real world to help me connect education with practice.

Pearl of Wisdom

"To be a social worker is to be in the relationship business. The most effective way to help another person is to build a meaningful, genuine, professional relationship with them."

~ Jeremy Carney

ABOUT THE AUTHOR

Dr. Jeremy Carney is a Professor of Social Work at Minnesota State University Moorhead. His research interests center around ethics and professional relationships in social work practice. Jeremy's professional practice experience has included child protection services, work with runaway and homeless youth, and mental health care. When Jeremy takes off his social work hat, he is active in officiating youth and college athletics, traveling as far and wide as possible, and reading good science fiction & fantasy novels. Jeremy is married to Jennifer Heath, and together they have two adult children, Ian and Katie.

Around Social Work

Here you will find journeys shared by those around social work. You will hear from a few professionals within fields around social work such as education, psychology, and business consulting services. Social work is a collaborative profession, relying heavily on its closest partners to influence and collaboratively move the serving professions forward in thoughts, words, and deeds.

MICHAEL MCKNIGHT, M.A.
SPECIAL EDUCATION

TOWARD A PEDAGOGY OF BELONGING

TEACHING a troubled child is the consummate teaching experience, the ultimate challenge for your abilities, the perfection of the teaching art. It would seem unfortunate to teach for twenty years and never have a truly troubled child in your class to test your abilities.

"Of course, no one ever said it would be easy- but perhaps no one ever told you it could be this rewarding either." – L. Tobin (1991)

I come to this project, not as a social worker, but rather as a teacher. I taught what our system continues to call 'emotionally disturbed children and youth' for fourteen years, and then became an administrator for a program that worked with troubled young people here in New Jersey for a little over a decade. After my on-the-ground experience, I worked with the New Jersey Department of Education and had the opportunity to learn from many school districts in the state. I am currently an adjunct professor at Stockton University in New Jersey where I get to teach future teachers as well as providing professional development to practicing educators. My goal is to shift schools toward trauma responsiveness and inspire deep educational change. I am thrilled to have an opportunity to share with you what these young people have taught me over the decades.

After graduating with a degree in Special Education with a concentration on working with emotionally disturbed students, I began my teaching journey teaching a self-contained classroom in a middle school setting. By early October of that year, I had hit rock bottom. The young people I was hired to teach were out of control every day. I was in constant conflict with these 12 young people and struggling to get through the day. Most days could have been described purely by arguments and anger. I found myself unable to sleep through the night, waking up early every day and unable to get these children out of my thoughts. I would find myself wishing that a few of them would not be in school the next day, hoping that I might be able to "control" the others if my major problems were absent. Of course, my most troubled students came every day. I was literally in conflict with middle school kids from the time they arrived until the time their bus came to take them home. The principal at the school told me very early in the school year to keep those kids out of his office! I attempted to do this work for two years, with very little success. During my second disastrous and painful year, I went back to school to get my master's degree in special education. Again, I was hopeful that I could learn something to prevent me from failing as a teacher. But I found the program focused mostly on behavior modification, point systems, and other forms of external control that really caused more problems than they solved. By then I knew that I needed to try something else.

"TROUBLED kids are distinguished by their regrettable ability to elicit from others exactly the opposite of what they really need." – L. Tobin

Albert Bandura was quoted as saying that fortuitous events have more to do with what happens in life than formal plans or processes. While watching the news one evening in 1980, I saw a clip about an organization that was running wagon trains with delinquent youth called Vision Quest. I contacted them, and shortly found myself and my future wife —a social worker—on our way to Arizona to work with adjudicated adolescents. At the time, I was just looking for anything that would allow me to escape my lack of success in the classroom. Little did I know that the experience would change my life's direction.

"THE MISBEHAVIOR of troubled children is seldom what it first appears to be. Understanding this, I believe, is the only place to start. No child has a need to create a life of conflict."
– L. Tobin

At that time, Vision Quest was a private residential program working with adjudicated adolescents who came directly from jail into the program. I became the special education teacher, but what I learned did not take place in the classroom. There was always a need for more coverage in the group homes where the young people lived, so in effect I had the opportunity to live with troubled adolescents. I was involved with helping them prepare dinner, clean up, do their homework and chores, and became involved in some free time activities prior to bed. I would stay over many nights to get the adolescents up, out to breakfast and on to school. It was literally a 24/7 experience. For the first time I was also able to sit in on some of the group counseling that was done and hear about these young people's lives. Their histories and their pain were literally heartbreaking. My now wife and I would also have the opportunity to take some of these young people on their home visits. In my first two years as a classroom teacher, I would read the evaluations of my students, but often did not connect the dots of these various reports. Now, living with and hearing about their lives, I was able to begin to understand that there was deep pain underneath all these young people's surface behaviors. Beyond the pain, I was able to see and experience the incredible resiliency of these kids. This experience was my first threshold crossing that began my journey that continues to this day. Today, I find myself at a stage in life where I am able to share what these young people allowed me to learn with both practicing educators and future teachers.

"THE HURT that troubled children create is never greater than the hurt they feel." – L. Tobin

Now some forty years later, our culture continues to mass produce troubled children and youth. A quick scan of the state of children in America performed annually by the Children's Defense Fund revealed that, in 2020, a public school student is suspended every 2 seconds, a child is arrested every 45 seconds, a child is confirmed abused or neglected every 48 seconds, a public school student is corporally punished every 49 seconds, a baby is born into poverty every 1 minute, a child is arrested for a violent offense every 12 minutes, a child or teen dies by suicide every 3 hours and 11 minutes, and a child is killed by abuse or neglect every 5 hours.

What *is* encouraging is that more and more professionals are aware of the Adverse Childhood Experiences (ACE's) study originally conducted by the Centers for Disease Control and Kaiser Permanente in the mid-1990s by Dr. Vincent Felitti and Dr. Robert Anda. This study linked adversity in childhood to propensity for negative outcomes in life. The more adverse childhood experiences a person had in their life showed links to a higher risk of physical, cognitive, emotional and social problems as an adult. Since the original ACE's study, many other similar studies have been conducted. (Felitti V. J., 2002).

In 2017, Dr. Wendy Ellis, now Assistant Professor at The George Washington University and the founding Director of the Center for Community Resilience, developed the "Pair of ACE's" that expanded upon adverse childhood experiences and connected it with "Adverse Community Environments". Adverse Community Environments include: high levels of community violence, high cost of housing, poverty, discrimination, lack of opportunity, economic mobility and social capital, and community disruption. Recently Dr. Ellis has added Covid 19 to the adversities faced in communities. (Ellis & Dietz, 2017)

Added to these ground-breaking studies, we are now also learning more about other forms of trauma across historical trauma, racial trauma and inter-generational trauma.

Trauma breaks relation. As Deb Dana (2018), a clinician and author who works closely with Dr. Stephen Porges and his work with the poly-vagal theory, states: "Trauma compromises our ability to engage with others by replacing patterns of connection with patterns of protection."

As practitioners, our work begins when we recognize that our most difficult, troubled, and troubling children and youth are kids in pain. They carry within their bodies toxic levels of stress and trauma. James P. Anglin first described the concept of "pain-based behavior" in 2002 (Anglin, 2002). Pain-based behavior is triggered by the re-experiencing of deep-seated psycho-emotional pain. Physical and emotional pain share similar pathways in our brains. These young people will act out externally on others, internally on themselves, or a combination of both. They are in a persistent state of alarm and will act out their pain externally on others, internally on themselves, or a combination of both.

Dr. Gabor Mate (2019) puts it this way: trauma is a Greek word meaning 'wounding'. Trauma is an embodied experience. Trauma is what happens inside of you as a result of traumatic events. Mate often speaks about the need to establish safety in the healing process and states: "Safety is not the absence of threat; it is the presence of connection."

Bessel van der Kolk (2015), in his book *The Body Keeps the Score* states: "The loss of the ability to regulate the intensity of feelings is the most far-reaching effect of early trauma." In his work, van der Kolk goes on to say that developmental trauma will impact behavior across multiple domains spanning emotional dysregulation, behavioral dysregulation, attentional dysregulation, somatic dysregulation, relational dysregulation, and identity disturbances. Broken relationships are at the heart of developmental trauma.

As people tasked with supporting children and youth who demonstrate pain-based behavior, our ability to deal with their primary pain without inflicting secondary pain through punitive and controlling reactions is central to our efforts. We must be cautious not to address "pain-based behaviors" with pain-based discipline! Troubled children and youth do not respond to our schools' various techniques of punitive discipline. In fact, school discipline procedures can make things worse, not better. There is a tremendous need to shift how we view discipline away from the use of punishment and toward our ability to co-regulate the students' emotions. Co-regulation is how humans develop the ability to regulate their behavior over time. Children and youth learn to self-regulate over time through attachment to caregivers. As humans, it is important to know that there will be an ongoing need for co-regulation for our entire life span. We are feeling creatures who think. We are neurobiologically designed to respond to one another.

In a conversation with a colleague, Dr. Frank Fecser, he talked about how "one of the greatest benefits in working with troubled children and youth is that you get to live at the edges of your competence and discover that they are not fixed."

There is nothing easy about this work. Troubled children and youth carrying toxic levels of stress and trauma into our schools often have learned to associate adult interventions with adult rejection. Emotions and feelings are very contagious, and troubled children will stir up feelings within adults trying to support them. These feelings can be uncomfortable at best and at our worst, if unrecognized, can get the adult to act out. Unless the adult is aware of how the trauma and stress is affecting the brains and bodies of those they work with, it can trigger in them unconscious feelings that in turn will lead to making them feel rejected, proving them right.

Aggressive students can trigger our fight/flight/freeze/fawn response and we can become counter aggressive or afraid.

Educators and administrators may think, *"This kid gets so angry, he is so frightening, he is crazy. He is out of control and dangerous. We can't handle him here!"*

Withdrawn and depressed students can leave unaware adults feeling helpless and providing less and less attention and care to these kids.

Educators and administrators may think, *"We have tried everything. She never does anything. She does no work and often seems to disappear in class, her hood up, her head down. Half the time she tries to sleep in class. I give up on this one."*

Traumatic stress and trauma in children and youth can often look like attention deficit hyperactivity disorder (ADHD). These young people do not have ADHD. Toxic stress and trauma result in children and youth being stuck in a state of persistent alarm. They are always on edge and do not feel settled in their bodies. If the adults working with them learn to pay attention to their own bodies, they will recognize that they reflect the feeling, almost like they drank too much coffee!

In these cases, educators and administrators say things like, *"This child needs to be medicated. He cannot sit still, cannot pay attention, cannot even remember things he knew yesterday. He's all over the place."*

Dr. Nicholas Long, a mentor that is now in his nineties and retired, co-author of *Conflict in the Classroom*, as well as *Talking with Students in Conflict,* and founder along with Frank A. Fecser of the Life Space Crisis Intervention Institute developed the conflict cycle. The Conflict Cycle describes the dynamics of the struggle troubled children can become involved in, and the way adults can intervene, protect the relationship and use the conflict as an opportunity for connection and growth (Long et al., 2014).

"The more healthy relationships a child has, the more likely he will be to recover from trauma and thrive. Relationships are the agents of change and the most powerful therapy is human love." – Bruce D. Perry (2017)

Many intervention strategies for working with troubled children and youth are focused on changing the surface behaviors of these young people. But behavior change does not start with things we change in kids. Behavioral change starts with us the adults.

Our learning can move in different directions. We can learn from the latest cutting-edge research coming out of the world of neuroscience, as well as learning from some of the ideas of pioneers that have worked in the past with troubled children and youth. It is a great time to be a learner.

And as educators, we do not need to become therapists to be therapeutic.

Dr. Nicholas Hobbs (1982), once the president of the American Psychological Association wrote about the concept of the "teacher/counselor" way back in 1982. Hobbs saw a need for educators to integrate some of the skills counselors and therapists learn into teacher education. For example, integrating personal calming strategies can help educators, as Dr. Nicholas Long states, "Be a thermostat not a thermometer." We can become aware of our personal "buttons", the things we are sensitive about and decide not to get hooked when a student activates one of our buttons. We can also focus and improve our ability to listen. Listening involves attending skills, reassuring skills, affirming skills, and validation skills. Using these skills, we can learn to help troubled children and youth bring language to their emotions. These "therapeutic listening skills" help us to build connections with relationship reluctant children and youth. The use of "I" messages rather than "YOU" messages to connect and calm children having a stress response also is a therapeutic skill that can be taught to all adults in a school community. Learning skills like these will allow adults that work with young people to co-regulate their behaviors. Relationship building with your most troubled kids is an endurance event and requires from adults a commitment to not give up.

These skills are important for all school staff as they move their school toward becoming trauma-responsive. These skills are great for all children. Trauma-responsive school environments benefit every human connected to the school, including the students' families and community.

"Education is always a vocation rooted in hopefulness." – Bell Hooks (1994)

Along with some of the therapeutic skills that were mentioned earlier, there is one I would like to add, albeit less technical: the therapeutic power of kindness.

My mentor, Dr. Nicholas Long, wrote an article twenty-five years ago, in which he was thinking about the therapeutic power of kindness. In it he speaks about kindness as being a vital therapeutic force to our well-being and our work with troubled kids ((Long et al., 2001).

In my mind, kindness is related to empathy and compassion.

Carl Rogers (1980) defines empathy this way: *"The state of empathy, or being empathic, is to perceive the internal frame of reference of another with accuracy and with the emotional components and meanings which pertain thereto as if one were the person."* The listening skills mentioned previously are important for educators to get a felt sense of understanding the inside perspective of the student. Listening well provides psychological air and is the first step to building connections with troubled children and youth.

Once we have a felt sense of the inner world of a young person, compassion asks us to act. Compassion is an emotional response to empathy. Compassion is a response to suffering. Compassion is an inner experience and it can lead us to act inwardly with ourselves or outwardly toward others in an effort to alleviate pain. My favorite definition of compassion is: ***"Compassion is a relational process that involves noticing another person's pain, experiencing an emotional reaction to his or her pain, and acting in some way to help ease or alleviate the pain"*** (Kanov et al., 2004).

Compassionate teaching starts with kindness. Kindness involves caring for and about the students you serve. Kindness is our ability, regardless of student behaviors toward us or others, to always treat children and youth with dignity and respect. Kindness is a way to demonstrate to young people that we care. Troubled children are resistant to relationships, for good reason. Kindness allows us to meet their needs for predictability, structure and routines, to set limits on their behaviors when necessary and pass their "trust tests". By demonstrating kindness in an ongoing manner, we slowly build trust and trust is an essential part of our work with these young people. Trust allows for the feeling of belonging and attachment to occur which are a critical component of growth and healing. As another mentor of mine, Dr. Larry Brendtro, states in his book, *Deep Brain Learning*: **"The need for trusting relationships is as basic a need as hunger or thirst."** (Brendtro & Mitchell, 2022). What our most troubled and troubling children and adolescents need are transformative relationships. This is the heart of our work.

Pearl of Wisdom

"View your life through the lens of kindsight. It is OK to make mistakes, that is how we learn.
View other human lives using the lens of kindsight.
Kindsight allows connections and connections lead to care, safety and healing for us as well as the young people we serve."
~ Michael McKnight

ABOUT THE AUTHOR

Michael has been involved in education for over 40 years. He has worked as a teacher, an administrator and as an educational specialist for the New Jersey Department of Education. Michael was a special education teacher for 14 years working and learning with emotionally and behaviorally troubled adolescents. Also, he served as an administrator at Atlantic County Special Services School District for 10 years where he was responsible for the programming for troubled students, ages 5 thru 21 years, who were removed from the local school district.

Michael is also an adjunct instructor at Stockton University in New Jersey where he teaches classes on inclusive education.

His current passion is working with schools interested in becoming trauma responsive.

Michael is the coauthor of two books: *Unwritten - The Story of A Living System* & *Eyes Are Never Quiet - Listening Beneath the Behaviors of Our Most Troubled Students.*

19

BETH TYSON, M.A.

BECOMING AN EXPERT BEGINNER

When I chose to become a counselor, I thought I was doing it out of a deep desire to help other people, to rescue them from suffering. But, along the way, I learned that this work would save me and give me a place to feel at home. Since you are reading this book, I'm willing to bet that inside of you lives someone who needs a place to call home, and I hope our stories inspire you to join us.

Before having my daughter, I was a family therapist working alongside the child protection department. My role was to stabilize foster, kinship, and adoptive families on the verge of having a child removed from their home. Today I am a CASA volunteer for two children in the foster care system and the author of *A Grandfamily for Sullivan*, a children's book inspired by my work with kinship families.

When I first stepped into social work, a veil was pulled back, revealing a world that a girl from Maine had never witnessed before. Early in my career, I referred to what I saw behind this veil as our society's "underbelly" or shadow side. But now I see it as the result of psychological trauma passed down from generation to generation, through systemic racism, learned behavior and epigenetics. Prior to my experience as a counselor, I questioned how anyone could lose their child to the foster care system until I became a mother and realized just how slippery the slope truly is. Without a support net to catch me and the many other privileges of being a white woman in the United States, I could have easily ended up at the bottom of that slope, unable to care for my child. I now believe that most children end up in the child welfare system because their parents live with untreated trauma and mental health challenges, which often leads them to self-medicate with drugs and alcohol.

Pearl of wisdom: Untreated childhood trauma can lead people to self-medicate the uncomfortable symptoms of anxiety and depression they experience after tragic events. This trauma creates a "cycle" of trauma that is passed down to future generations.

I was born with the safety nets of sober, employed parents with the emotional wellbeing to care for me, guide me, love me, and keep me safe as a young child. That's not to say I grew up without any struggles because we all have them. But I believe that being born into my circumstance is a privilege not bestowed upon everyone. As I became an adult, even my safety nets didn't prevent me from struggling with my mental health. Still, when I needed help, I could access it, which is not always possible for people.

I grew up happy by my standards and didn't feel sad very often, but my childhood was punctuated with loss and adversity. At the time it all just felt "normal" to me, but in my twenties, I began to experience panic attacks and unhealthy relationships with other people. These experiences prompted me to stop wondering what was wrong with me and look back at my life experiences to consider what happened to me.

I was born and raised in rural Maine, and my parents divorced when I was two. I lived full time with my mom, older brother, and mother's boyfriend, who I refer to as my "stepdad," even though they never married. On holidays and over the summer, my brother and I traveled to Long Island, New York, to spend time with my dad and my step-mom. They also visited us in Maine when they could, which was always a special time together, but generally home life remained disjointed from the start.

I had two homes located about seven hours apart and in significantly different environments from one another. Even as a happy little girl eager to spend time with my family in New York, I remember these transitions being difficult for me. As you can imagine, I missed my mom and the familiarity of my home in Maine. Where my New York family lived was very busy and suburban compared to my life in Maine, and this was hard to adjust to.

Despite the difficulties in their relationship, my parents always did the best they could for us. I always felt that they loved me even though they couldn't make their marriage work. Because I was only two at the time of their divorce, I have no memories of my family being intact. As a mother now, I often wonder how they made it work. The stress and grief of shifting two young children back and forth between New York and Maine sound gut-wrenching to me, but they did it for the right reasons. That meant I grew up knowing they loved me but with a frequent sense of "ambiguous loss" and a longing to be in one place when I was in another. To be clear, I don't blame anyone for these circumstances because they made me who I am today: a warrior for children, as my stepmom would say.

Although we had some adversity, we also had protective factors or positive childhood experiences (PACEs) to mitigate the impact of that adversity. Thanks to my parents' and step-parents' hard work, I grew up in two financially stable households. We lived in predominantly middle-class neighborhoods with adequate resources and education. And in addition to all of this, we had Maine: a haven of nature, awe, and endless inspiration. In Maine, I was enveloped in a peaceful cocoon of trees, fields, creeks, lakes, blue skies, and the smell of insects and milk-weed, which kept me grounded. One afternoon, I laid down in the grass in my backyard and locked my eyes on the fast-moving clouds above me. I laid there, still, alone, for what seemed like forever, watching the clouds drift by and listening to the sounds of the wilderness. I felt small and insignificant compared to the universe, which was comforting to me. It meant I wasn't responsible for it "all"— whatever that meant.

Another protective factor in my life was my big brother and step-sister. At three years older than me, they were the ones who were always there for me no matter what. We frequently spent our free time walking horse trails in the woods of Maine with our German shepherd by our side as a guide and protector. When I was alone, I would write. I kept a diary and created books with short stories. Despite the challenges within our family, I mostly felt at peace with my life, and I believe these protective factors mitigated the impact of the disruptions in my early life.

Pearl of wisdom: Protective factors like one supportive caregiver, community connections, and time spent in nature mitigate the mental health impact of childhood trauma. Relationships heal.

There would be more adversity to face as I neared my teen years. We moved a couple of times which unsettled our family. When I was about eleven years old, we moved to New Jersey and left my stepdad behind. The end of this relationship meant another ambiguous loss for me to grieve without any acknowledgment. Leaving Maine was upsetting for me, but I made it work. Soon I was creating a new life despite my anger and sadness. However, moving to New Jersey significantly changed my mom. I think she thought our moving would make our lives better, but she found it difficult to secure employment nearby. She was traveling long distances in heavy traffic both ways to work. Some nights she came home crying and went straight to bed. It was a hard time for all of us.

As I adjusted to suburban life, my mom began to focus on her dating life, a new experience for me to witness. My mom had provided a very stable, loving home life in Maine, but now she was acting out of character. She often got involved with untrustworthy men and left a string of boyfriends in her wake, which became troublesome for our family. I worried about her safety, and I never knew what trouble she might be in next. So I kept it all inside and focused on my friends and finding a boyfriend of my own.

I listened as she struggled with her dysfunctional relationships for the remaining days of her life. We existed inside of an inverted relationship, one where I sometimes took on the role of a responsible adult while she became more child-like. Parent-child relationships like this can leave unintentional wounds on the psyche of children. At the time all I knew was that my mom needed help, and I wanted to be there for her.

Pearl of wisdom: My inverted relationship with my mom was an example of parentification, the term for the psychological damage that occurs when an adult caregiver leans too heavily on a child for emotional or functional support. You will frequently encounter parentification if you work within the child welfare system.

In retrospect, I think my mom was suffering from untreated depression about the family life she had so desperately hoped for but never achieved. She might have turned to chaotic relationships to distract herself from the uncomfortable emotions she was feeling. In contrast to my mom's description in my teen years, she was also an intelligent, creative, kind person. She was my biggest cheerleader, and despite her mistakes, I am endlessly proud of her for all she endured as a single mom of two kids. She taught me how to persist and never give up. Although I questioned her mothering when I was a teen, becoming a mom made me realize just how much she sacrificed for me. Her mistakes didn't stop my love for her and never will.

Pearl of wisdom: Children will continue to love their parents no matter what they do.

In 1997, I started college, but I still hadn't declared a major by the end of my sophomore year so I met with my academic advisor. She noticed that I had already accrued many credits in psychology through my chosen electives. She suggested I follow my natural interests, and she was right. I remember her asking me "What do you read about in your free time?" I replied, "Usually articles about people, behavior, and psychology." After that discussion, I chose to major in communications with a minor in psychology. However, I graduated in 2001, still not knowing what I would do with any of it.

Pearl of wisdom - take a look at your natural interests. What calls to you despite whether or not someone tells you to do it?

In the summer after graduation, I applied for a job I found and was hired as an executive assistant. Three months after starting this position, 9/11 happened. At the time, my brother was living and working in lower Manhattan near the World Trade Center. My family spent the entire day unable to get a hold of him and fearing the worst. Eventually, we found out he was safe, but shortly after this horrifying event, he decided to leave the smoky remnants of lower Manhattan to take a position in sunny California. His move was yet another ambiguous loss I would have to face—this time without him.

Perhaps my early experiences with ambiguous forms of loss were gingerly preparing me for my most painful loss, my mother's death. When I was twenty-six, I still spent a couple of nights a week at my mom's house, even though I had my apartment in the city. With the summer of 2005 winding to an end, I headed to my mom's one morning to go shopping. When I got there, she said, "The strangest thing happened last night; I went out dancing, and when I came home, I fainted for a few minutes." Having all the maturity of a twenty-six-year-old, I said, "That's really weird mom, but it's probably nothing," and we went on about our day. Two nights later, she died in her sleep from a pulmonary embolism. Her dying so suddenly meant I didn't get to say goodbye. I didn't tell her I forgave her for her mistakes, and she would never meet her grandchild. She was gone forever.

My mother's death is the most significant turning point in my life. Although she died in her sleep, her death awakened a powerful drive in me. It was a recognition of the finitude of life at a time when my adult life was just beginning. Most people numb or repress the reality of death, but this realization was like turning on the lights in a very dark room for me. For the first time in my life, I felt motivated to make a difference in the world. Until that point, I was doing well. Life was pretty stable but also directionless.

The loss of my mother created an urgency to live my life purposefully. I knew spending my time in a corporate office would be like dying a little bit each day instead of living. And I had to live now before it was too late.

I decided to look into a career change because I had a knowing that I was meant for more. So, I took a chance on myself (and several loans) and worked full-time while going to graduate school at night. With each late night that passed, I knew the love I fostered had found a new home in helping others. My degree took me four years to complete and the help of one very supportive future husband. Finally, I graduated with a master's degree in clinical counseling at thirty-four years old.

Two weeks before graduation, a classmate asked, "Have you found a counseling position yet?" Sheepishly, I replied, "No." I was still working at my internship and enjoying the energy of a college counseling office. I thought my goal was to secure a position in counseling at a local university. But my classmate said, "The non-profit I work for has an opening for a family therapist. I could give you a recommendation if you are interested." So, of course, I took her up on the offer. A month later, I became an in-home family therapist for foster, kinship, and adoptive families within the child welfare system. To say that I was nervous was an understatement. I was fresh out of graduate school, not a parent yet, and with a long history of disrupted relationships. How would I be a good family therapist for children with a history of trauma and loss? But I knew a higher power was calling me to my home, and I was heading in the right direction.

The resistance I felt starting as a therapist was strong. I doubted myself frequently. Coming out of graduate school, I thought I would feel confident, but instead, I felt inadequate. What helped me most through this anxiety was the community around me. My professors, teaching assistants, and new supervisors encouraged me to continue. Their belief in me sustained me when I didn't trust myself. They reminded me that I wasn't taking the role of a therapist to "fix families" but rather to guide people towards growth. One day, I had a meeting with my supervisor about one of my clients and said, "I don't feel like I'm helping him enough. I feel like I need to give advice and answer his questions directly. What if my client won't participate in another session?"

My supervisor responded, "There's always the chance he doesn't. But giving him the answers will rob him of the growth that can happen when he solves the problem himself."

As therapists or social workers, I learned that our job is to help our clients become autonomous, which means we help them develop a sense of capability in their lives. If you give a person advice or too much help, one of two things will happen: they will either attribute any success they have to you, or attribute any failure they face to you. Neither of these outcomes is helpful for the client or the therapeutic relationship.

Pearl of wisdom: It is essential to question your desire to rescue people. What if we steal their best learning opportunities when we save people from their struggles?

I went through extensive training at this non-profit and spent hours in supervision talking about my fears of inadequacy. Over time, I realized that I didn't need to be a parent to do family therapy and I also did not need to be an expert to be successful. My personal experience with grief and loss would allow me to understand these families on a level that most people never would. Most importantly, I got comfortable with the idea that my only job in the beginning was to hold space for the client's pain. The families I worked with needed to feel heard and safe before they could even consider the steps to move forward with their children.

Pearl of wisdom: Listen with the intent to listen and not the intention to problem solve. The amount of trust between you and your client is the best indicator of success.

One night I was driving home from a tough session, and I called my dad in tears: "Dad, I want to thank you guys for all you did for us growing up. I don't know where I would be without your support." Since my mom was no longer alive, I sent the same message to heaven. My experience in social work led me home, to know myself better, to understand my family's struggles without blaming anyone, and to trust my ability to support people through their trauma and loss.

Pearl of Wisdom

"People who want to help others typically put a lot of pressure on themselves to be perfect, but it's necessary to allow yourself to be a beginner in social work. You are not required to be an expert to do this work well, it will take many years to hone your skills, all you need is to be curious about why you really want to do this work. Remember, the people you meet on your journey into, around, and possibly out of social work will teach you more about yourself than you could ever know about them."

~ Beth Tyson

ABOUT THE AUTHOR

Beth Tyson, MA is a childhood trauma consultant, and children's book author. She has several years of experience as a mental health clinician working with families impacted by trauma. Beth provides education and training to organizations who want to prevent and heal childhood trauma.

Beth is a Court Appointed Special Advocate (CASA), a member of the CASA Advisory Council, and a Voices for Children Coalition partner, advocating for youth impacted by trauma in the child welfare system. She is also a professional member of the Pennsylvania Counseling Association.

Most proudly, Beth is the mother of a courageous little girl with a very big heart and a secret chocolate stash in her room, just like her mama.

Website: BethTyson.com

20

THU-HA PARK

YOU CAN DO ANYTHING IF YOU PUT YOUR MIND TO IT!

HAVE you ever felt a pitted hunger in your stomach—one of hunger and worry about the next meal? Fear of not knowing what you would walk into at home? Have you ever kept yourself so busy that you couldn't think of the pain that could happen next, or felt completely uncomfortable in your own skin as if your body wasn't your own? Have you lived your life in darkness wondering if it could get better? Or why God hated you so much as to put men in your life that would only either leave by death or destroy any sense of life that lived inside you?

A sense of belonging wasn't something I easily found or felt for myself. I was inadequate at home and I felt displaced at school. With only a few other Asian students, I attended grade school with predominantly Caucasian Americans who were from fairly well-to-do families. My friends were always in ski club, camping, traveling, and having the newest and greatest things. My Asian friends told me I was too white because I spoke proper English. I was targeted in school and teased for being the girl who brought lice to school just because I had black hair. I was separated from my regular class schedule and put into English as a Second Language class when English was actually my primary language.

In 1980, my parents had made the difficult decision to leave their families behind and were sponsored to the United States. The all-American dream became a difficult life, and being labeled as refugees from

Vietnam came with stigma and discrimination. During their escape the year before from Vietnam to Malaysia, my dad was informed he was sick with leukemia. In 1988, he opened the first Asian grocery store in our area, and within six months he lost his fight with cancer. My mom couldn't receive benefits and was left with a devastating financial burden.

My mother's cry for my dad on his death bed has never left me; "ông Lieng!". I remember holding on to my dad as he lived his last minutes of life and thinking, "If I hold on to him tight enough, maybe he won't leave me." Unfortunately, I was wrong. I can still remember how his hands felt so big and safe, and how his fingers wrapped between mine. They felt safe. I've only experienced the feeling of being safe a couple of times in my life with men. But it would all quickly fade and leave me feeling "not loved". I often find myself chasing the illusive feeling of 'safe' with men and find disappointment in the short-lived moments still to this day. Although I had a beautiful relationship with my dad, that wasn't the case for all of us. After an eye-opening conversation with my sister, I realized our memories of our dad were actually of both a protector and an abuser.

After my fathers's death, my mom worked hard, working several jobs to raise six children on her own. She had three boys and three girls. The middle brother, Tien, was like a father to me and I would later leave college to run his business. While living at home, he would always take me to do things and eat at the local restaurants. We enjoyed traveling together. I remember we were in Mexico, and I wanted to give up on snorkeling because the water kept seeping into my mask. He came up to the surface with me and worked with me until I agreed to go back down. He never left my side in the face of fear. Little did he know that the times we spent together were my reprieve from my other brother's beatings.

My family was feeling the pain and financial challenge within the home. I would open the refrigerator door to find an empty fridge except for an orange juice container of drinking water. At five years old, I was already cooking and quickly learned to fend for myself by stealing clothes, food, and everything and anything I could get my hands on for survival. Stealing and fighting was my ticket into the legal system. On one of my last visits with the judge, he said, "This is not the path you are meant for, I don't want to see you back in my courtroom".

I took the words of someone who believed in me and never looked back.

After my father's death, one of my brothers became my abuser. I thought I was trying to escape the pain of physical abuse, but years later, I realized that it had been the verbal abuse from him that stayed with me. I wanted to be anyone but me. I can still hear him say, "You're a f*cken idiot, you're so f*cken stupid, no one will ever want to marry you, you can't do anything right, no one will ever love you." These harsh and cruel rebukes had become the biggest restraints on my ability to exist. Locking myself in my room provided the only sense of safety and peace. I managed my pain by watching and learning how to dance like Janet Jackson and Jennifer Lopez. I sang songs by Whitney Houston and the Little Mermaid dreaming one day of becoming a singer. Back then, I wanted to be anyone, but me.

Growing up, the relationship with my brother was violent and unpredictable. The smallest infractions would trigger his violent behavior. From accidentally drying his jeans to not getting all the wrinkles out of his shirt, he would use physical abuse to show his discontentment. He did not respect women and engaged in sex and drug use. Because of his habits and uncontrollable temper, I lived in constant anxiety, fear, and chaos. One of the worst beatings was when I called my sister a 'whore'. I am not sure if he was defending her or because he didn't like the word. Nevertheless, I was punched in the head so hard that I landed across the room. With each encounter, he would scream and tell me to pick myself up and look at him. That night, I took a handful of pain medication, went to bed, and hoped I would never wake up. Unfortunately, it was not my time to die and I woke up with a horrible headache and nausea. I just wanted to die.

To avoid going home to an abusive household, I engaged in after school activities throughout my elementary and junior high school years. I joined the drama class, played in the school band, performed in plays, and played in sports just to be away from home for three more hours. I was voted to be in the student council and quickly failed to uphold my responsibilities. I did not attend the meetings and couldn't stay sober enough to care. I hated life and everyone around me. By the age of 13, I was already engaged in drinking alcohol, cutting, smoking, stealing, and bulimia; all things that I was able to control. It was my way of feeling safe.

My destructive behaviors became my ideal safe place. I started my day with a shot of vodka before school, then another in between classes to get me through the day. I often would sneak into the woods behind the school grounds to drink just before my after school activities. I continued to push the limits of my alcohol abuse and numb myself from the world around me. Nothing could stop me, not even a bad hangover from the Gray Goose brand vodka; which later became my best friend and enemy. I wanted more control and something to take the pain away. I was not sure if I wanted to live or die. It felt like a battle that would never end.

Child protection came into my life in eighth grade. The abuse from my brother was finally reported. I was interviewed by workers, removed from the home, but then I was given unsupervised visits. I was sick to my stomach with both excitement and fear. Even though my brother was my abuser, I was excited to see him because deep down inside I still loved him. I feared not being perfect, not making someone else happy, and mostly I feared being unlovable. I hated myself. When he hugged me, I never felt safe again even though I desperately wanted to feel loved and protected. I was allowed to move back home, but moved in with a friend instead. After a while, my mom talked me into moving home and convinced me that he had changed. Within six months, he started beating me again. With no one to protect me, I packed a few bags and called for a ride. Between thirteen and eighteen years old, I was homeless. I lived out of my car, couch surfed, stayed with my then boyfriend, and eventually lived with a friend and manager before leaving for college. I'm still not sure how I even got into college.

Thinking back to high school, my drinking and grades had taken a turn for the worst. I regularly took shots in the back of the bus on the way to school and had a 64 oz Super America cup filled with vodka and orange juice. I was always drunk during Spanish class and did not care if I did well or not. My teachers did not seem to care either and my GPA was at 1.9 at one point. At that time, I was living with a friend and she sat me down to administer some tough love talk. Our conversation had me briefly stop my drinking habit just enough to get my "shit" in gear to improve my GPA. Through the Post-Secondary Education Option Program, I completed my requirements at a local community college and I graduated high school with an associate degree. Despite my academic achievement, I still drank 1.75 liters of alcohol a day and had thoughts of suicide.

I was accepted into the University of Wisconsin-Eau Claire and left for my college experience in 2000. Life was going right for once and I was excited just to be a normal college student. During my junior year, I was accepted to study abroad in Edinburgh, Scotland and was happy to be fulfilling my dream of world traveling. Unfortunately, that dream came to an abrupt halt and my worst fear happened. My brother Tien was diagnosed with stage four lung cancer and was given six months to live. At that time he was running a successful restaurant called the Grand Junction, which later he renamed Tinn's Philly Steak Subs, and needed my help to keep the business open. There was no hesitation in my decision to leave school to help my brother with his business.

My brother was a fighter and learned to live with his illness. His six months prognosis turned into 13 years of constant chemotherapy treatments, hospital visits, surgery, and sickness. Living with Tien's cancer became a new normal for our family. I often became angry at him for not resting at home. He would respond with, "What am I supposed to do? Should I just sit here and wait to die?". I felt his courage in his voice, and from that point on, I've never doubted his intentions. I was able to run his business for 9 years and obtain my bachelors and master's degree.

Just as quickly as I felt driven to be a therapist, I quickly was discouraged to not become a therapist. My practicum (clinical field experience) supervisor told me that I was not meant to be a therapist and I should pursue a different career field. As a young student working on her self confidence and budding career, I took her feedback to heart and had a severe second thought. Could she be right? Fortunately, two people I met during my practicum experience encouraged me to continue forward with my dream.

Fortunately, two beautiful individuals were on my path at this time, and told me to continue moving forward. They believed in me. Before finishing my program, I reconnected with my former undergraduate professor, Dr. Biscuit, who was able to validate my experience and knew of the interpersonal conflicts this supervisor had with others. She knew ever since I was in her class that I was meant for this field and told me to reconnect with her when I was licensed, but fear and shame took over. Instead of working through this, I planned to leave and travel the world for seven months through Kenya, Vietnam, Kathmandu and

India before coming home. I was working four jobs at this time. I saved all my tips, spent my checks on bills, and saved the remainder. I left the country without any intent of getting licensed, but rather thought I'd take over Tien's business with my then best friend. My brother's kidney started failing so I cut my travels to four and a half months. I lived in anger until my time in Kenya when beautiful people introduced me to love, kindness and passion for life and helping others. I finally found some purpose! Kelly, Lexi, Kia and Erico believed in me!

I came home and we started working on a new Tinn's location, but the plan fell through and I went back to the idea of licensure. I connected with Dr. Biscuit about places to start my internship, and with the next three calls, I was sick with anxiety and fear of rejection. Here I was, vulnerable again. She believed in me, and that was enough to conquer my fear of failure.

In 2014, my brother, Tien, lost his battle with lung cancer and passed away. He was the one man in my life that truly supported and loved me unconditionally. His passing stopped my world and I was angry at God for taking him away. I asked God, " Why would you take the one person that I felt safe with?". I felt alone and struggled to cope with the loss. Tien loved being around people and knew how to celebrate every accomplishment. He was the type of guy who was there for you morning, noon, and night. My favorite memory of my brother is when we drove to Atlanta, GA for Hot Import Nights. He loved racing cars and we all shared in his passion for them. My family and I would joke that he would "kidnap" us when doing a quick errand and would return us back home hours later. I will never forget the day that he put a Prelude H22A motor in my Honda. It was his way of showing how much he loved me. It was called a 'sleeper' because you could not tell by looking at it that it was in fact a pretty fast car. Yes, the thought of running a ¼ mile and watching the movie, *Fast and the Furious* still brings me excitement. He was not only my brother, but my mentor, protector and someone who always believed in me.

It's difficult to fully understand someone unless we know their story and provide a safe environment for them to share. I've been given an opportunity to share mine and bring hope to people. I've struggled with my decision to be in the social work field, but found passion for it through my own journey. I will admit, there are times when the emotional aspect of my job can be a lot to digest and I felt like not returning to work. The one instance that made me think about not returning to work was with an adolescent patient, we will call him "E", who completed suicide. I felt it was my responsibility to give him hope to live. The trauma E experienced might have been more than I can help him with and it was a difficult situation to process. During our time, he would say, " sometimes I just need you to listen, you don't have to solve something". It was the last words he would say to me and it was a great lesson to learn from.

Processing trauma is never an easy thing to go through. Even at the age of 38, I was cued during a group therapy session that I was leading. My clinical director, at that time, did not understand my experience and was dismissive. She said, " But he didn't actually touch you." As a trauma therapist, I thought she would have validated why that situation brought me back to past trauma. At that point, I knew I had to stay in the profession to advocate for people with physical and verbal trauma experience.

My position as a Licensed Professional Clinical Counselor gave me the platform needed to start my advocacy for marginalized populations. I am fighting for those who are not seen or have not been heard. I want to give voice to those who feel their culture(s) do not support them. My goal is to reach the Southeastern Asian community and break the cultural persecution and taboos about mental health. At the same time, I want to approach the topic in a way that honors their culture and the subculture in which they live. I hope to change the field of psychology and how therapists provide care. Ultimately, I am working towards empowering others to break free of intergenerational trauma. I want to walk alongside them in their journey toward change and provide hope, to meet them in their own light or darkness.

The moment I stopped my self-destructive behaviors, life began to open up opportunities for me. My pain became the fuel that allowed the lost, insecure girl inside of me to dream of building an empire, to be inde-pendent and to have empathy for others. I am blessed to be given the opportunity to share my journey of struggles and journey of healing. Nowadays, my escape involves getting lost in nature and being surrounded by water. I am reminded by the sunrise and sunset to look beyond what we see on earth and to travel the road less traveled. Your story doesn't have to determine your future, but is a road map to over-come any adversity. My story is about coming out of darkness and giving hope to those who do not see a way out. I was told that I was not meant to be a therapist and have proven that all wrong. I gave myself permission to live and enjoy what life has to offer. And what life has offered me are two beautiful boys who remind me how important it is to take a moment to enjoy the present, to make memories, to love further than the moon, and to surround yourself with others who lift you up and love as hard as you do. Life is too short to spend it with people who don't see your value. I've been fortunate to have several people on my journey who BELIEVED in me.

Pearl of Wisdom
"Be the one to believe in someone else, for this could be the reason they conquer."
~ Thu-ha Park

ABOUT THE AUTHOR

Thu Park is an MS, LPCC/Certified DBT Clinician/EMDRIA EMDR trained mental health therapist. She has been in the mental health field for 7 years and currently works in private practice. She is passionate and committed to helping people explore their needs and meet them where they are at in their personal journey. As a practitioner, she focuses on trauma work and the individual healing process. She works with a diverse population (BIPOC, LGBTQIA+) and continuously advocates for inclusion in her methodology. She is a mother of two curious and adventurous young boys who keep her extremely busy. She is an avid world traveler who took five months after graduation to explore different cultures. To recharge from her day-to-day, she loves to be outdoors fishing, hiking, camping, and chasing sunsets at Lake Superior-Northern Minnesota. She hopes to pass along her love for world travel and the outdoors.

LinkedIn: linkedin.com/in/thu-park-84872b97

21

WARREN L. GRAVER, MBA, PMP

THE VILLAGE INSPIRES THE BEST IN US

IMAGINE HOLDING to a pretense that you were raised by grandparents, aunts, and cousins, while your mother was off attaining tertiary scholastic achievements. I firmly held this notion, because my earliest recollection of family entails vivid memories of my grandmother, her home, and other family members. My mother passed away over a decade ago, which has raised my conscious being of self, family, and ancestry. Fortunately, ancestry.com and connecting with cousins who I previously hadn't known have connected dots where I knew not those dots existed. During this search of my heritage, I have learned that despite my high melanin pigmentation, both my maternal and paternal great-grandfathers were of European descent. But I digress. In a recent conversation with a cousin who is more of an older brother, I asked, "What year did my mother depart to study abroad, leaving me with our grandmother?" Bemused, my cousin queried the existence of that thought, as my mother's educational obligations were long completed before my arrival into this world. The response taught me a lot about the village, its impact on me and the necessity of it in nurturing, supporting, and protecting a child. The depth and boundlessness of my village during my germinal years somehow created this incorrect notion of my mother not being present. Then again, it's quite possible that her presence was overshadowed by my grandmother, who remains the epitome of unconditional love. My grandmother was the wealthiest person I knew, burdened with a luxurious disposition of compassion, empathy, and love. Her wealth extended beyond the petty presence of materialism and embodied everything that we should all aspire to be: unconditional in our delivery of love and respect. In spite of the numerous challenges she encountered in her long life (she lived into her 90s), she remained stoic and always seemed to find the positives regardless of life's challenges.

The presence of my *patois*—or as my American friends and associates will say, Jamaican accent—doesn't support the fact that I have resided in the United States for the majority of my life. Raised in Kingston, Jamaica with my mother, stepfather and two brothers (one older, one younger), I departed Jamaica in 1993 to pursue a bachelor's degree at the prestigious Howard University in Washington, DC. My goal then was simple and straightforward: complete a Bachelor's degree in business and return home. I failed miserably. Somewhere along my academic journey, I managed to become married to the idea of pursuing advanced degrees. This led to attaining my MBA that would be followed up later with a Masters in Information Systems Management. These were accomplishments that, if I am being true to myself, were once deemed unattainable and impossible. My quest for knowledge and aspirations to be better were in stark contrast to the misguided adolescent who left Jamaica with luggage filled with uncertainty. My high school tenure was abysmal to say the least, and my unfortunate grades were merely a reflection of my lack of effort and noncommitment to my education. Not surprisingly, this unfortunate experience served as a major strain on my relationship with parents who were very much academically inclined. My misery was further compounded by my high school PTA President being none other than my mother. Despite my dismal school performance and the stressors it caused, I was surrounded by a support system that saw value in someone who could have easily been written off as meritless. The village ensured that my immaturity would not hinder my destiny of fighting the good fight.

I consider myself to have been raised in a normal Jamaican household in a middle-class family. And although my parents were divorced, I was not raised in a broken home. As best as I can recall, my stepfather had always been in the picture. We had an absolutely great relationship. He had an easygoing personality, while my mother was primarily the disciplinarian. It was much later in life that I learned she was quite the comic, and perhaps I would have learned this sooner if only I had upheld my part of the educational bargain. But that was always going to be a challenge. You see, the education system in Jamaica is as challenging as they come, and differs significantly from the American education system. For starters, there is no middle school. Most students attended a preparatory or primary school until the sixth grade, and then they were off to high school. The transition from elementary level schooling to high school required successfully completing the Common Entrance Examination (although the requirements may have changed since my days). I attended St. Cecelia Preparatory school. It was a small private school, where discipline was strictly enforced. The only available sport was table tennis, and our main recognition came from producing quite a few Spelling Bee champions. I like to believe that my academic downfall started with the transition from preparatory school to high school. Upon successfully completing the Common Entrance Examination, I was presented with an opportunity to attend Jamaica College (JC), one of the most prominent all-boys high schools in Jamaica. It should have been an easy transition; not only did my older brother attend JC, but so did the majority of my peers from the neighborhood. As a public school, JC offered the intersection and immersion with children from diverse demographical and socio-economic backgrounds. JC stood out from all other boys' high schools, because while the other boys' schools wore khaki brown uniforms, JC wore royal blue shirts and navy-blue pants. Upon reflection, I suspect this experience of standing out is one of the reasons I am now comfortable living in Maine.

Attending JC was the single most catastrophic period in my life, but at the same time it offered valuable life lessons and experiences that to this day have an impact on my approach to passions and relationships. Transitioning from a small preparatory school to JC was a recipe for mayhem. For starters, I learned that attending classes was mandatory, but staying to the end was optional; I chose the latter on most occasions. There were also many options for sporting activities, and I learned playing in uniform was informally acceptable. My sport of choice was football (though Americans call it soccer), and I pursued every opportunity to play. Or, so I thought. I was terrible at it! In a moment where perception and reality were misaligned, I attended tryouts for the school's Under-13 squad. It did not go well, and the onlookers were merciless with their commentary. There were strong suggestions that my cleats should be relinquished to someone else who could use them appropriately. And that is putting it mildly. Apparently,

I was a glutton for punishment, because there were several other tryouts that ended with the same result. Representing JC was simply not in the cards. But while I struggled athletically and was noncommittal academically, socially, school was a great experience. In the midst of the toxicity that manifests at an all-boys institution were the lessons on friendship and empathy. The strange dynamic at JC was that enemies on the school grounds were brothers once off the campus. We were truly our brothers' keeper. The classmates who were less fortunate and from a challenged socio-economic background were often assisted by those who had the means. In a high conflict environment with the presence of an abundance of alpha males, there lived compassion. If I left JC with anything substantial, it is the lifelong friendships that still exist to this day.

After my high school tenure, much to my parents' chagrin I spent a year and a half "soul searching." I like to believe this time was necessary to unpack all that I had experienced in high school. And while my parents' thoughts on this time may have differed, I suspect they appreciated later that if that was my worst moment as an adolescent, it was better than many other potential avenues. In the midst of the badgering on what I was doing with my life, I eventually opted for evening classes to attain the subjects necessary to work or attend college. Equipped with a different mindset, or perhaps with my back against the wall, I found success this time around. With credentials secured and the assistance of a neighbor, I was able to land a job and a sense of purpose. After a year and a half of finding financial independence through gainful employment and at the urging of my parents, I decided to explore attending college. In 1993, I begrudgingly migrated from the warm isle of Jamaica to pursue a business degree at Howard. Begrudgingly, because my preference was to attend St. John's University in Queens, New York. St. John's was within walking distance of family, and I was also familiar with the neighborhood. At the time, I was unable to correlate my disastrous high school transcript and the negative impact it had on my postgraduate aspirations. If only my parents had articulated the significance of my high school education to me! But alas, they did; I was simply too immature and not focused on long-term goals to understand their message.

If JC brought damnification, then Howard brought redemption. Its impact on me wasn't realized or appreciated until many years later. Affectionately referred to as the "Mecca," Howard is a prestigious historically black college or university (HBCU) that personifies black excellence. It's an environment that boasts high caliber minorities, burgeoning to make their impact on the world. My acclimation to Howard was not as easy as expected, likely because I was transitioning into independence at the same time as living in an unfamiliar foreign country. In hindsight, my transition should have been easier than I experienced, considering the abundance of Jamaicans on campus. There were also quite a few of my associates from JC, along with the almost twenty cousins who I shared the campus with. My first semester was subpar academically, but I otherwise enjoyed a stellar academic experience. Not only did I blossom academically, but I also managed to graduate with honors and made the Dean's List in six out of the eight semesters. In addition to my academic success, I also earned a roster spot and represented Howard's varsity soccer team as a walk-on.

My years post Howard were somewhat nomadic as I sought to find my professional passion. The journey took me to an import/export business, the hospitality industry, and a short stint with a family-owned engineering consulting firm. None of these stuck. Unsettled, I found myself returning to Jamaica in 2001. Unfortunately, the Jamaica I saw was not the same Jamaica that I had experienced growing up, and I opted to return to the US. A rekindled relationship led to a union that produced two wonderful children, a daughter and a son. Sadly, the relationship was short-lived and the marriage eventually dissolved. In hindsight, the divorce in itself was not traumatic; I have learned to appreciate the possibility of people growing apart, or habits and culture making a relationship unsustainable. The traumatic experience was having to navigate three of the most daunting experiences a person can encounter at the same time. Not only was I experiencing a divorce, but I also learned my mother had developed breast cancer; this was further compounded by me losing what I thought was my dream career. It was also during this time that I had my first interaction with social services and the unjustness of the justice system. I was not prepared to experience the disregard for fathers and the notion that fathers are incapable of caring for their children. The entire experience left me frustrated, angry, and with a strong disdain for child protective services. Despite the ruling—or better yet, opinion—of the 'misjudge, I was still Dad, and my purpose and priority remained making every effort to love my children unconditionally—even if from a distance and on a schedule.

If I could have predicted the outcome of my 2009 Mother's Day trip to

Jamaica, I would have opted to travel earlier. However, I surmised that the gravity of being cancer-stricken was lost on my mother, and she had no interest in a pity party. Despite being immobile and confined to a wheelchair, her sole complaint was the inconvenience caused by her newly blurred vision. As an avid reader and the Queen of Scrabble, her cancer had metastasized and had impacted her vision, leaving her unable to read for leisure. What remained intact was her sense of humor and wittiness, which provided respite for my acknowledgment on how fleeting the life is that we are living. Here I was, a divorced Dad experiencing the theory of retrogenesis. Despite the circumstances, I reveled in the opportunity to be my mother's caretaker, including the backrub that lasted well over thirty minutes. Because, in spite of the numbness in my arm, I realized this was a small favor that could likely be a last request. My mother meant everything to me. She was both my protagonist and sounding board for navigating life. Looking back on my missteps through life, I somehow believe she knew where I was heading, long before I had any sense of direction, and allowed me to fall but not too far from the path. On Monday May 18, 2009, my mother rested peacefully but was with us no more. In the midst of my emotional state, I kept hearing her voice in my head: *"Warren, you don't have anything constructive to do with your time?"* She had always been very candid about death, and had opined that the tears should be saved for the living. As the news of her passing was shared, so started the numerous telephone calls. And while the callers were all despondent, dismayed, and in disbelief, I started gathering a recurring theme. The sympathizers all shared stories on difficulties they have experienced, and my mother's willingness to help without a second thought. The collection of experiences made me pause and reflect, and it ushered in a sense of pride. This was followed by an epiphany: while she was no longer here in the physical sense, her compassion, thoughtfulness, and contributions to the village would live on eternally.

Before I present my illation on what indirectly brought me to social work, I should share that in 2008 my then-girlfriend Victoria brought me on a trip to her hometown of Freeport, Maine. I couldn't explain it then, but there was something about this quaint town that compelled me to desire relocating there. This was the furthest thought from her mind, as she was enjoying the diversity of Washington, DC, as well as the mild winters in comparison to Maine's. Victoria and I met while playing soccer in DC, and have been inseparable since our first date on

June 28, 2008. After getting married a few years later and being blessed with identical twin boys, we made the decision to be closer to her family and relocated to Freeport. That unexplained feeling I had was the reminiscence of the village filled with love and caring neighbors that I had grown up with in Kingston. Shortly after we relocated, my eldest son joined us and my college-aged daughter decided to also make Freeport her home.

My career aspirations were primarily to serve in a management consulting capacity. I have been fortunate and blessed with the opportunity of working for two of the most prominent global consulting firms. While these firms boast a penchant for diversity and inclusion, the competitive environment and the absence of compassion led me to having imposter syndrome. After decades of navigating the corporate world, I sense that many professionals are struggling in "great" careers that are misaligned with their internal fire. Then came a turning point in my career. I was implementing software for child welfare agencies. Gathering business requirements from caseworkers and observing how they interacted with families in need changed my perception of the how and the why of the decisions they are tasked with making. That disdain I had for child protective services evolved into empathy. I have learned that they too are navigating this challenging system founded on outdated principles that has resulted in social workers being tasked with transporting water in a wicker basket; a task that is impossible. What brought me to social work and has compelled me to be a part of the solution is an understanding of the importance of second chances; I am a living testimony. As my journey from Kingston to Freeport demonstrates, I didn't always get it right and there were numerous course corrections required. The constant for me has always been the village, the helping hand, the people who inspired and cared. I have openly acknowledged my belief that social workers are superheroes, and whether they are aware or not of this recondite fact, they are the nucleus of the social services village. Through their compassion and commitment, they have inspired a nomadic technologist to get involved and explore avenues for being a part of the solution for improving outcomes for families; by mentoring at-risk-youths and crafting career development programs for youths emancipating foster care. I firmly believe if given the support and resources, social workers have the intellectual capability and lived experiences to strengthen our communities. The acts of compassion and support from the village are instrumental and necessary for anyone to mature and, ultimately, find the best representation of themselves.

Pearl of Wisdom

"A village doesn't always have to be family, and a village doesn't always have to be friends. As long as there is compassion, the village will inspire even the wayward to ultimately find the best version of themselves. A village isn't perfect; it has its imperfections — but as long as the compass in compassion is present, there will be guidance and an atmosphere of caring; and that level of support is as perfect as it can be."

~ Warren L. Graver

ABOUT THE AUTHOR

Warren Graver is a Jamaican expat who resides in Freeport, Maine with his wife, Victoria; along with their four children, Kayla, Alexander, and twin boys, Greyson and Jamison. Professionally, he is a public sector consultant, leading states and local government agencies through process optimization and technology improvement projects. Warren is the Child Welfare Practice Lead for BerryDunn, a consultancy based in Portland, Maine. He has extensive experience in the health and human services space. Warren is also an advocate of inclusion practices, and has led diversity business resource groups.

Warren's passion for child welfare led to him forming Social Retrospective LLC, an advocacy collaborative focused on guiding adolescents transitioning from the foster care system.

Warren is an alumnus of Howard University, where he attained his Bachelors and MBA in Business and Organizational Management. Warren mentors at-risk youths through the Seeds of Independence organization, and is also a youth soccer coach.

LinkedIn: linkedin.com/in/wgraver

Out of Social Work

Now we wrap up with a glimpse into a few journeys out of social work. Social work is a system. Systems are built with boundaries. Some journey stories do not fit within conformed boundaries, and to push boundaries to widen, you need to have boundary pushers. The journeys out of social work will invite you to consider such things as, social work's influence on the innovation of new integrative therapeutic strategies or that social work could even be an interior design strategy! System boundaries are no match for a heart on a mission!

2 2

DEB FRANK, MSW, BCTMB

WALKING IN THE FOG WITH MY BARE FEET

Ms. MILLNER WAS one of my favorite teachers in elementary school. She had a loud laugh and a goofy side that she wasn't afraid to show. The day she did a James Bond-style diving roll in the hallway after school was probably the first moment that I secretly admired her. Her extravagant personality mirrored her fashion sense. I was envious of the bohemian style clogs that she wore with her denim dresses. My short, chubby, pre-pubescent body was going through a transition phase that required oversized, baggy shirts that were too long in the arms, and rolled-up pants with an elastic waist and small pockets barely large enough to fit two quarters. Although I never disliked any of my teachers, Ms. Millner was truly a gem. She wasn't like the conservative Catholic motherly types that I usually had. She had confidence; she had power; and, she was the perfect distraction from my life at the time.

I grew up in a quiet, all-white Central Minnesota town where there were two distinct groups of people: Catholics and Lutherans. City blocks were small, and all of our backyards melded into one. For the most part, we lived a very typical day-to-day life. We spent every waking moment playing outside with our friends until it was time for dinner. Despite having fond memories of swinging from the clothesline and playing in the sandbox, it was particularly difficult for me as the oldest of seven children. I was the one who was ultimately responsible for the wellbeing and whereabouts of my sisters and brother, and if something happened to one of them, I would often get chastised. The parenting style of the 70's and 80's was different than it is today. We were spanked, beaten with a belt or wooden spoon, and slapped across the face so hard it would leave marks. My parents were like most parents of that era. They had hopes and dreams for their kids, but lacked the support, skills, financial resources, and awareness to change. I know my parents loved us, and they did the best they could. In fact, my conscious mind knows that they are the products of a much harsher generation. It's my unconscious mind that I still have yet to fully convince. Growing up within this paradigm has forever changed me.

Trauma took many forms back then. It was shaped like a dark, humid storm cloud during moments of family loss to suicide, cancer, and illness. It was a grey, foggy twilight at age nine when I fell off my bicycle and fractured my temporal and parietal bones. I experienced a near-death event and suffered chronic headaches and severe concussion symptoms as a result of the head trauma. Back then, nobody wore helmets and brain injuries were treated with a get-up-and-brush-it-off style of treatment, which was a reflection of how most things were handled. Truly, life had always been predictably unpredictable. Our family themes were chaos and emotional drama-trauma mixed with laughter and close connection. During some moments, the sky appeared to be a heavy, dark, blinding fog, while others were translucent and sunny. The memories of my childhood are not cataloged by dates or words, but by a string of emotions that I have embodied like a time capsule.

The year I had Ms. Millner as a teacher, I wrote a poem titled "Walking in the Fog with my Bare Feet". We were tasked with writing a collection of poems using alliteration and haiku. She assembled all of our poems into something resembling a book using an old-fashioned typewriter, a folded piece of construction paper, and two staples. The front cover was simple yet inspiring – just like our poetry. Ms. Millner had written the title of my poem on the front cover directly above a rusty brown signet. It looked sophisticated, and I felt important. What I hadn't realized at the time was how profound that moment was for me. She had embossed a feeling of worth and value into the deep recesses of my core.

My identity was so intertwined with my caregiving role within my family that I oftentimes felt a lack of clarity of who I was as an individual. Just like oldest children in large Catholic families back then, I was gifted a truck load of guilt and shame. So, walking in the fog with my bare feet was essentially how I navigated my life: feeling my way through the fog of ambiguity while grounding myself to the earth one step at a time. Eventually, I got really good at it. I splashed in the puddles and listened to the rain pouring down, as the poem suggests. I learned how to find joy and happiness in attracting new experiences and meeting new people. My view of the world had widened, and continued to expand with each diverse encounter.

College wasn't on my radar until a month or two before applications were due my senior year of high school. I was having a lot of fun exploring my independence that year and didn't have much guidance when it came to making sound decisions for my future. I had applied to a school I had never visited that was ten miles away. Thankfully, I was accepted, because this girl had no backup plan. Declaring a major in college was similar in style. I nearly failed my Egyptian Mathematics course, so I steered clear of anything that had to do with math. Social work became the most logical fit. I had absolutely no idea what I would do with a social work degree, but I did know that I was good at helping people.

Initially, I had dreams of joining the Peace Corps after graduation. It would be my ticket to travel the world! I attended introductory meetings at our local library and had all the paperwork filled out and ready to be submitted. The only thing standing in my way was the 9-lb. 14-oz. bundle of joy that was unexpectedly about to arrive. At the age of twenty-two, I was about to embark on the most course-altering yet meaningful experience of my life: motherhood.

The resilience that got me through my childhood was nothing compared to what was needed for this next leg of my journey. I was about to have a biracial child with a man who was unwilling to be a partner and a parent. In order to cover up my fear and pain, I would sometimes joke that I was preparing for my big debut on *Days of Our Lives*. The abridged synopsis in the *Soap Opera Digest* may have read something like this:

In today's episode of *Days of Our Lives*, Dr. Marlena Evans and John Black are about to have baby Belle at the Salem Hospital. In blinded love and intense labor, Marlena learns that John is really Roman Brady. In complete disbelief, Dr. Evans pushes through her physical and emotional pain as she is faced with the decision to stay with Roman or walk away from the lies and secrets that have yet to unfold. Marlena's life is about to twist and turn with Hope, Bo, Victor, and Stephano waiting for Belle's arrival.

My life felt like a damn soap opera. It felt like the only thing differentiating me from Marlena were my added themes of racism and single parenting, and Marlena's glamourous head of hair.

My first social work job after college was both challenging and exciting for me. I was relieved to have found someone who would hire me in my third trimester and was proud of not feeling like a complete failure. The only catch was that I had a position that required a lot of me. I was a live-in foster care provider for a home that provided nursing and foster care to medically fragile children. I lived in the basement with my son in exchange for cleaning the house and being on-call in case of emergencies. I also worked full-time managing the home by shopping for groceries and supplies, helping with nursing care, coordinating family visits, working with the county, and supervising part-time foster care staff. What I hadn't realized when I was hired was that I would be stuck in the middle of a power struggle between two agencies over the care and wellbeing of the children. After a year of challenges and frustrations, I gave my notice but immediately was countered with an offer to manage a different house that needed a strong leader. Again, with no back-up plan, I decided to accept the position.

Over the course of several years with this company, I continued to weather the storm from one foster care home to another and took on additional responsibilities. The company was expanding so quickly that the workload trickled down much faster than the pay. One evening after putting my son to bed, I remember feeling absolutely exhausted. I was done! Done with work! Done with parenting! Done with life! It was just too much for me. Resilience had morphed into a compromise with my sleep, my happiness, and my financial security. I knew I had to change my job, because my job was changing me.

Once again, I found myself in a hazy fog tiptoeing the ground below. This time, I felt a strong desire to take the path that led me back to school. I was so burnt out from systems, hierarchy, and constant change from my social work position that I yearned for something new that would provide a sense of calm and stability. I thoroughly enjoyed the medical aspects of my program coordinator position: changing and suctioning tracheostomies, cancer and end of life care, physical and occupational therapies, and medication administration. Yet, I despaired at the thought of entering another systems-based career. After careful consideration, I decided to become a massage therapist. I credit my friend, Stacy, for the inspiration. She had gifted me a certificate for a massage. Not only was it a transformative experience for myself receiving the massage, but I could see myself helping to transform the lives of others.

Leaving the social work profession wasn't like ripping off a band-aid quickly. It was a far more gradual transition. I continued with my current position as a program coordinator while attending massage school. My supervisor wasn't ready to let me go, and convinced me that if I simply "lowered my standards" I would be able to manage both. She was right. I delegated as much as I could and got done what needed to get done, and nothing more. Lowering my standards was the only way I was able to transition from one career to the next. But, when I'm all in, I'm all in! So, I knew I desperately needed to leave the field. My ethical standards did not align with the system I was in, and I was not in a healthy place mentally to be able to manage that anymore.

As a single mom, I needed the income that my program coordinator position provided. I didn't have the luxury of a second income earner who could support me while I pursued other endeavors. I had student loans, a car payment, and a young child to take care of. I honestly don't know how I managed, but I did. I was a master at getting by. After graduating from massage school, I knew I wanted to start my own business. Being self-employed would give me the freedom and flexibility that I desperately needed. I found a clinic that had a room for rent, and I immediately began advertising. My business was in operation for almost a month before I had my first client. That was a moment I will never forget.

I was at the clinic wearing a soccer T-shirt, a pair of red Umbro shorts, and my flip flops. I was organizing my therapy room and printing off labels to send out postcards. A man walked in, asking if I was open for business. He had terrible back pain from an auto accident and wanted to get a massage as soon as possible. Even though I was sporting a backyard BBQ vibe, he did not care. He was in his seventies and was hunched over from pain. He came back the following week for another session and raved to his friends about how much relief he had felt from that first massage. I gained an enormous amount of confidence and professional wisdom that day. People were ready for me; I had to be ready for them.

My business rapidly took off, and I knew it was time to finally cut ties with my social work job. I fortunately was able to move in with my parents for almost a year to help with the transition. I could not have survived the first five years of my son's life without the support of my family. He was the first grandchild and was spoiled beyond belief. He brought an element of joy and connection, as well as a real-life opportunity to further deconstruct my and my family's conditioning around parenting styles, gender norms, racial bias, and religious beliefs.

The two decades that followed my move out of social work were some of the most significant years of my life. I met a remarkable man who became my life partner and role model for unconditional love and who wasn't afraid to dismantle his own archaic, conditioned beliefs. After spending many back-breaking years expanding my business model that included employees and a second clinic, I finally learned that if I wanted the fog to lift, so to speak, I had to redefine self-worth, success, and leadership. If I wanted to feel more joy and synchronicity with life, I had to do the work to make that a reality. So, I closed my doors and moved my practice to our home. Working from home allowed me the freedom and flexibility to add more of the things that matter most: time with myself, with people, and nature.

This career shift has been critical in helping me learn more about my work. I filled my professional toolbox with a variety of holistic modalities and self-development classes, which enhanced my understanding of the inseparable connection between the mind, body, and spirit. I discovered a simultaneous shift in my clients as well. A massage therapy session became less about muscle tension reduction and more about spiritual discovery. When I allowed clients the space for emotions and thoughts to surface, their bodies changed in a way that I had never palpated before. I would get feedback about how deeply changed people had felt. Each session was completely different based on the depth that people desired. The co-created, sacred work that was unfolding in my therapy room had profoundly altered my professional lens. It felt exhilarating to unearth latent trauma and stress within a client's soft tissue and help them connect to spirit. Yet, the therapeutic process still did not feel complete. Being present with my client during their beautiful moment of clarity without having the skills or scope to come full circle with the experience seemed unfortunate. All I could do was refer them to a counselor for psychotherapy. So, in hopes that a Master's Degree in Social Work (MSW) would be that final ingredient I was looking for, I decided to go back.

Just like a spiral that gradually expands as it moves, so have I. My graduate experience has illuminated pathways to so many inspiring people, new thoughts and ideas that have both challenged and added to my own, and a deeper connection to the intangible aspects of myself that have yearned for expression. When I began my graduate studies, the vision in front of me was to create a professional model that truly embodied a mind-body-spirit approach to therapy: an integrative professional identity that combined psychotherapy, massage therapy, and spiritual healing. However, while researching the professional attitudes around an integrated model, I discovered many barriers. There were fears around touch, boundaries, licensing, and safety. I was also advised to maintain two separate practices. Certainly, putting this model into form was, and still is, unchartered territory. Traversing new land requires strength, courage, vulnerability, and the right timing. I continue to explore and ponder ways to navigate these barriers. Unfortunately, each new idea that sparks excitement and hope has been followed by a gentle reminder that I cannot sacrifice my own quality of life in the process. The healing work that I currently do brings me joy and fulfillment. So, until tides shift, I will continue to walk on the beach with my bare feet waiting for the right wave.

My professional journey has mirrored my personal journey in so many ways. Because of this, it is difficult to ascertain if I am in, around, or out of social work. Truthfully, I view the terms 'social work' and 'massage therapy' more as action words that are integral aspects of my identity as a healer. Each profession has given me the tools, language, knowledge, skills, and wisdom to do my work. Still, my work as a healer is much broader than that. Being a healer means that I both deconstruct and construct thought; I continue to learn how to love myself and others unconditionally; I use my voice to promote justice and meaningful change; I help others in my community who need support; I work to end generational trauma; I nurture the earth; I strive for peace; and I continue to help humanity thrive. My identity as a healer has not changed, but the expression of my work continues to evolve every day. Likewise, the story of the little girl who walked in the fog with her bare feet does not end here. Her legacy has just begun.

Pearl of Wisdom

when I walk
in the fog
with my bare feet,
I splash
in the puddles
like this:
s-p-l-a-s-h !!
and when the rain
comes down
it sounds
like this:
d-r-o-p, d-r-o-p !!
~ Deb Frank

ABOUT THE AUTHOR

Deb Frank has been an integrative massage therapist, Reiki master and teacher, personal and professional coach, and trainer for over 20 years. She also has a master's degree in social work. Deb applies a strength-based, holistic model, rooted in social work philosophies, to her healing practice. Deb's extensive and diverse education, training, and experience help to provide each individual with a personalized session that promotes healing. She considers her role as one that creates awareness, facilitates change, and holds space for others to do their own work physically, mentally, emotionally, and spiritually. She believes that no two people are alike, and therefore no two sessions are alike. Deb lives in Minnesota with her husband and son. She and her family enjoy kayaking, camping, hiking, traveling, volunteering, and connecting with family and friends.

Website: www.debfranktherapy.com

23

AMANDA FORDHAM

THE POWER OF INTENTION

Part 1

MY STORY BEGINS at thirteen years old; a freckled-face young girl whose body was changing and hormones had gone rogue. I was born to a mom and dad who loved me more than they loved themselves and whom I loved more than anything in the world. As the oldest of three, I was very much the cliche oldest child; responsible, perfectionist, worrier, and a natural born leader. I had so much to be grateful for yet I could sense that something was "off" with my parents...I didn't realize how "off" things were until one evening, on the way home from volleyball practice, my mom's voice cracking with emotion as she asked what I would think about her divorcing my dad. *Heart racing. Heavy breathing. Tears falling. Time standing still. Overwhelmed with uncertainty.* How could this be happening? How could my family be falling apart? What would this mean for my siblings and I? So many unknowns and so many questions raced through my mind. It was at that time that I truly began to understand the feelings of fight or flight. I knew I would have to fight for my family, especially my little sister and little brother, then twelve and seven. As time continued to stand still for me, the world around me would move quickly. Divorce. Two homes. Shared custody.

Although this is where my social work journey began, my full story began before I was even born. My dad grew up a strict, devoted Catholic and my mom had hardships within her family growing up. Coming from two very different worlds, after seeing those two pink lines, they discussed parenting styles and how things would look different than that of what they had both experienced. Out of those discussions came the decision that they would take a different, more laidback approach to faith and religion. They took a faith-based risk which allowed me the freedom of curiosity and left my heart cracked wide open for my own faith journey instead of having one chosen for me. I'm forever grateful for that faith-based risk; little did I know, I would need that higher power and freedom of curiosity to run to at thirteen years old. I would need that forever friend that offered comfort and hope. I can remember hitting my knees and praying to someone who I thought was named God, who I knew existed, but didn't yet know intimately. Do you remember your first feeling of needing or knowing God? Do you remember your first aware-ness that something bigger than you existed? All I knew is that I needed someone...something...to get me through this time in my life.

As a newly 'divorced kid' my parents put in a referral to the school social worker to check in one on one. The social worker's name was Katie and she was an earthly angel; she was kind, friendly and made me feel safe. She created a place of no judgment and total support. I also joined a peer-to-peer group with other kids my age who were going through tough times. In hindsight, it was my time with Katie and the group that made social work become a part of who I was, a part of my being. My story and the stories of my peers made me feel connected in a way that I hadn't been able to feel at home.

At home, I had stepped into the helper role, always putting on a brave face to ensure that my sister and brother's needs were being met. With Katie or the peer group, I could be vulnerable and get out my feelings of uncertainty. While at home, I had no other choice than to adapt to the helper role; it just became deeply and internally who I was. Over time, I developed this need to help others with suffering I understood. It pulled me out of the uncertainty and unknown; it allowed me to trust in the journey. I took on the 'mom role' at my dad's and the 'dad role' at my mom's. I had this strong desire to make our houses feel like homes, no matter who was in it. I remember constantly rearranging my room and my sister's room to make things feel as homey and comforting as possible; this love and passion for making a house a home has been etched on my heart for as long as I can remember. Maybe because this was something I could control? But it was also something that brought me joy!

Part 2

Years of surviving and even some thriving came as we settled into our new lives; bonus parents and bonus siblings came into our lives whom we loved, and my parents who were truly happy in their new marriages. Blended families were living their best lives...until they weren't. We are all born with different coping mechanisms; as I embraced the helper role, never allowing myself a reprieve from being that steady anchor, my sister fell hard into addiction. Her addiction to drugs became her escape, her full-fledged coping mechanism for unresolved trauma, and led to more trauma. What started as experimental use became her survival. She fell fast and hard. Through high school, my sister would use on and off and our relationship was strained. As committed as I was to the helper role, I didn't have what it took to fix this. *Heart racing. Heavy breathing. Tears falling. Time standing still. Overwhelmed with uncertainty.* How could this be happening? How could my family be falling apart again?

College was right around the corner, and every career placement test pointed to the helping professions. Because of the profound impact Katie had on me, social work felt like the path. I was ready and excited to start this next chapter; I chose a state university only three hours from home. It felt far enough away from my family to secure some independence. After years of taking care of everyone else, what I really wanted in life was independence, but not to be too far away in case anyone truly needed me. In hindsight, this was a strategic choice as it provided the power of choice, control and balance. It allowed me the freedom to trust in the journey of what was to come.

College life was great. I was only responsible for myself and I embraced every ounce of independence. I would meet and fall in love with the man of my dreams, my now husband, Chris. My girlfriends became family and I loved where I was at in life. I felt like I could finally breathe. I stayed busy decorating all the different homes I lived in throughout college, ensuring they had a homey feel. I loved everything about how design and decorating made me feel inside. My sister had periods of sobriety while I was away at college too, and she gave me my second love, my nephew, Collin. After graduation, I moved back home to pursue a career in social work.

Part 3

I started my career in the addictions field. About two years into my career, my little brother was in a very tragic car accident that left him with a traumatic brain injury. He was unable to walk and talk, and his independence was forever taken. *Heart racing. Heavy breathing. Tears falling. Time standing still. Overwhelmed with uncertainty.* How could this be happening? How could my family be falling apart...again? We were in what felt like the pit of hell on earth. Imagine being asked to say goodbye to your loved one to then having their life spared, then being forced to relive that grief and loss every time you are around them. The version you knew no longer exists. Somehow, by the Grace of God, I was able to get up each day and go to work, focusing on what I could control. That was putting my brokenness aside to pour into others. This gave me purpose and hope, and helped me to have trust in the journey despite uncertainty and heartache. I poured any extra energy I had into making our first house a home. I spent hours researching the latest design trends, taking on DIY projects one room at a time. Decorating distracted me from the pain I was walking through, this healthy distraction brought me joy, it made me feel alive. About a year later, I would be blessed beyond my wildest dreams with the promise of forever to Chris and the birth of our first daughter, Rylee Jane, who helped slowly fill the cracks of my broken heart. Grieving the uncertainty within my family just became a part of who I was and I tried really hard to not let it define me...until it did.

Just when I thought nothing could feel as bad as this grief, my sister fell hard back into addiction. I was settling into my new job as a child protection social worker. I threw myself into my caseload of chemically dependent parents, mostly moms. These were years of not knowing if my sister would live or die. Years of using, making and selling drugs. Years of breaking the law and wondering if she'd end up in prison. Years of working in the same child protection system that had an open case with my sister. My heart was cracked wide open for all to see what was going on in my family. I ran from those feelings and did the only thing I knew would help me to survive this unimaginable grief by helping others. I had this deep yearning to provide empathy and hope to others that were in a space that I was in. I remember thinking, "If I couldn't help my sister, I was going to pour every ounce of that heart space into helping other moms who were in the same pit of addiction." Little did my clients know, they were helping me as much as I was helping them. After all, my clients were someone else's sister and if I could help lessen that kind of pain, from one grieving sister to another, I was going to continue running after that healing. My family would grow by two more beautiful baby girls, my identical twins, Maysen Rae and Parker LeAnn. I would go on to have many deep connections with chemically dependent mamas on my caseload. I would spend time helping them turn their houses into homes. I would spend hours breathing new life into old, forgotten furniture pieces, believing in their new life and their newfound beauty. These furniture makeovers felt cathartic. They paralleled how I felt about my clients and their new lives and their newfound beauty. I found a balance that was helping me get through each day while also begging God to work a miracle in my sister's life—but a miracle doesn't even describe what happened next.

Part 4

This is where things get Godly! My sister finally hit rock bottom, on a cold, concrete floor of a jail cell. She, too, had a moment with whom she thought was named God, much like my moment at thirteen years old; she hit her knees and cry out for help: "God, if you're there and if you can hear me, I don't want to live like this anymore but I know I can't do it alone. I need your help, and if you are willing to help me, I will do whatever it takes to never be here again." Faith had always been behind us and never in front of us. We always knew God existed but never with certainty; maybe because it seemed our prayers hadn't been answered before. (Dear God, please bring our parents back together; Dear God, please fully heal our little brother.) It wasn't until this prayer was answered, in a way that was undeniably something only God could do, that our faith was fully in front of us. As my sister went through long-term treatment, she became healthier than we ever knew possible. She grew hungry for the Lord and became the best version of herself. She was oozing with joy, beauty and hope. She was the living, breathing testament to fully surrendering to faith. Her journey of sobriety, along with her intimate relationship with the Lord, left me to reevaluate my faith and my career; I was hungry for more too. I wanted to know Jesus the way she did. She quickly became someone I admired and sought to be like. I was learning that life was too short to settle for something that no longer brought me joy. *Heart racing. Heavy breathing. Tears falling. Time standing still.* I felt uncertain in my career but certain that we were both exactly where we were supposed to be; that all of the pain was a part of our journey to reach this special place. I felt freedom from this invitation to perhaps be released from social work. But it left me with big questions. What else would feed my soul? What else would bring me joy?

I would go on to add our fourth child, my sweet baby boy, Crosby James. After returning to my child protection role after my maternity leave, everything felt different. For the first time in my career, I had moms on my caseload that refused to let me in. They put every barrier in the book up, and it made coming to work each day difficult. I was drained, frustrated, and confused, because even in the hardest cases in my child protection journey, I had always made genuine, trusting connections with my clients. This was unknown territory for me. It made me feel uncertain and inadequate every step of the way. My heart was finally healing from the personal grief and pain I had gone through for years during my sister's drug use, and I now embodied the real-life testament that healing and sobriety was possible. In hindsight, I believe this deeply rooted 'aura' of hope, healing, and possibility I was proudly displaying actually became a roadblock for me and my clients. It must have been scary for a total stranger to believe in their future more than they believed in themselves. My personal healing and my sister's sobriety released me and led me out of my career in child protection. And my curiosity and trust in what was next would lead me to take the biggest risk of my life.

Part 5

My heart was ready to leave social work but my brain was not. I'm not a risk-taker by nature. While I didn't feel ready to leave social work, I felt ready for something that would give me more balance. I was starting to feel the emotional cost of this work. I transferred to Victim Services where I provided assistance to victims of crime. While this position gave me more balance initially—so much so that we would welcome our fifth baby, Finley Grace, into the world—I couldn't help but feel that uncertainty creep back in. I felt that my 'sparkle' for social work had started to dull, and I knew, through years of experience, that if I didn't keep my heart open for what God had in store for me next and fully trust the journey, I might miss out on something incredible. I prayed big prayers for God to restore my 'sparkle' and felt him asking me to just trust Him; to jump and he would handle the rest. I also felt him remind me that I had fought hard my entire life for my sparkle, and that by trusting him, he would renew it within me. Knowing my God-given talent of design and social work, I was at a crossroads of awareness, now with my faith fully in front of me, leading me to take the biggest risk of my life by moving out of social work to pursue design. I knew that God was paving a way for me to take my years of social work experience and wisdom and combine it with my passion for design to turn it into something special!

Spoiler alert: I am now pursuing design full-time. Currently, I'm the lead designer at a home-design-center where I help people from all different walks of life bring beauty into their homes. I spent over fifteen years pouring my heart and soul into creating safety and sobriety in people's homes. Now I get to use that heart space and energy in a very different way. I have no formal training; just a dream in my heart and a God-given talent that fills my cup. I can see so clearly now that God put design in my heart early in life *and* He led me through social work so that I would have the strong foundation of understanding people, the need and importance of relationships, and the power of intention. My goal is to turn design into something much bigger and more mean-ingful than just pretty spaces. I have adopted what I am calling "the social work design strategy" which means that even in an industry that is money driven, I will always care about the person before the product or sale. I will make them feel seen, heard and valued because that's the only way I know. While pursuing something that FILLS ME WITH SO MUCH JOY, I am also honoring the foundation that social work built. I have an awareness of what it means to turn a house into a home. I understand the deep importance of knowing the value of a home because I've seen people without them, unable to fill them or afford them. I know what it's like to live between two homes, and I'm now building my forever home with faith-based intention and a desire for people to feel and see Jesus when they walk through my doors. I want them to *feel* like they are at *home*.

Homes are more than just a space; they are our safe haven, a reflection of who we are and our legacy. I want to encourage you to evaluate what brings you true joy. What makes you sparkle? How cool is it that

God knows every inch of your being, every inch of your heart, every strand of hair on your beautiful head? He is so intentional. He is so creative. He is so loving to give every one of us such unique gifts, talents, passions and callings that make us SHINE. A fitting metaphor from snowy Minnesota says that snowflakes don't lose their sparkle; when they melt, they evaporate until it's their time to freeze and shine again in a completely different way. I'm grateful to be able to shine again in a whole different way; it will never be lost on me what a gift it is to leave a little sparkle wherever I go.

Pearl of Wisdom
"Do not settle within uncertainty. Have faith in the purpose of the journey, for the purpose of the journey will eventually lead you to certainty."
~ Amanda Fordham

ABOUT THE AUTHOR

Previously a social worker, Amanda has spent the last fifteen years pouring her heart and soul into incorporating safety and sobriety into people's homes – but for as long as she can remember, she has always had a passion for interior design. She is excited to now be pouring that energy and heart space into creating beauty in people's homes. She is a proud law enforcement wife and a mama to five littles; Rylee, Maysen, Parker, Crosby and Finley. On the rare occasion she has some down time, you can find her with an iced coffee in one hand and a paintbrush in the other, breathing new life into old furniture pieces. Amanda is grateful for her time as a social worker as it strengthened her relationship with the Lord, taught her so much about herself, resiliency, integrity and the importance of never giving up hope.

Facebook: Amanda Suzanne

Instagram: @amanda_fordham and @thefreckledpoppy

24

ASHLEY ABRAMSON

THE JOURNEY HOME TO MY INNER MAGIC

AT EIGHTEEN YEARS OLD, I fell in love; it was a deeper love than I had ever known, a love that felt so pure and protecting. When I saw him, I knew he was my person, the one I would dedicate my life to and ensure he never had to feel the hurt he had already in only his short months on this earth. I knew that, although I did not give birth to him, he was mine; our paths had crossed so that I could be his mother and protector. He is my dear son, Jaydon.

Eighteen years prior to feeling the deepest love I had ever known, I came into this world as a pure soul having a human experience. I was a child filled with curiosity, wonder and joy. I always felt an internal pull that I was here to have an impact on this world in a grand way. However, I didn't quite understand what that impact was. This sparked a constant sense of curiosity and wonder within. I was constantly questioning and testing the boundaries that this world presented me with.

As I grew older, the external world was not always welcoming of this questioning. I was often told that I talked too much and at times was seen as an instigator. This was confusing for me because my intention was so pure and truly came from my heart. Although I knew my intention was pure, over time I took on the external reactions from others and adopted them as my own. I felt like my curiosity and wonder were not acceptable behaviors and therefor I would need to conform.

Conforming for me looked like doing what I was told, never questioning why, and creating a life that resembled the people around me.

At first, living like everyone else was an adventure in my eyes. I was able to become a chameleon and take on the traits of others. As time passed, I started to lose my own light and it became dimmer and dimmer. I became more depressed and essentially bored with life. Adventure and learning are what I lived for; and at that time, they were unacceptable. As time passed, I started to question if continuing on this journey was even worth it anymore.

Fast forward to a year before I became Jaydon's protector, and I was the one in need of protection. I had made the decision to take my own life, and I almost succeeded. The doctors could not explain my recovery as I miraculously recuperated. At that time, I realized there was a plan for me much larger than I could ever imagine. I knew I was meant to walk with others on their journey—even though I didn't know exactly how to do that.

Jaydon was in foster care when I first met him. He was only five months old when I met him, and he had already been through more than most adults in his short time on earth. He always had a huge smile on his face and a beauty in his eyes like I have never seen. Meeting Jaydon and looking into his helpless little eyes, I knew that this was my purpose in life: to be there for him to provide him the human connection he deserved and what I didn't have. His father, my husband at the time, gained custody of him when Jaydon was eleven months old, and so our journey together began!

I again had a purpose and an outlet for my curiosity and wonder that was socially accepted. In advocating for Jaydon and his needs, I filled my inner child again. If I could not advocate for my own needs, I could instead utilize my skills of questioning, love and adventure to provide him with every opportunity I wish I had.

The time with Jaydon and working with some of the most beautiful professional souls in child protection is when I realized my career and my full purpose in life.

I decided I was going to be a child protection worker. I promised myself to do my best to make sure the children of the world were provided with the love, safety and stability they needed to not only survive in life but to thrive. I was here to ensure the safety of children through working with their parents. I provided them the support and hope that they did not have so that they could be the parents that could nurture and protect in a way they had not received.

My life was dedicated to the children of the world and their caregivers. Little did I know that this effort would be accompanied by heartache and deep connections that would be created in the process.

On August 30th, 2010, I officially started my professional career as a child protection worker. I was over the moon excited for all of the possibilities, human connection and impact I was going to have on this world. I was eager and ready to learn new ways to connect and provide support to the families I worked with.

Only a few days into my job, another worker who started on the same day and I were tasked with removing two teenage children from a home. They had a significant history of trauma prior to the current home they were in and were now unsafe in this home as well. We were short-staffed and we figured two newbies were equal to a seasoned worker, so we set out to "save" these children. No amount of schooling could have ever prepared me for this day. It was absolutely heartbreaking. We were not welcomed with open arms; instead, we were cussed at. The two teenagers emotionally responded as though they were toddlers.

The things these children had been through were only things I had seen in movies. We had only met them minutes prior to taking them from the home they knew and were about to leave them at a complete stranger's home. It was awful. One of the children loaded her things in plastic bags and the other in her beautiful suitcase. Seeing the emotional damage inflicted on them and my inability to provide them the comfort they needed in that moment left me crying all night long. This was the first of many more times that I would enter a child's life as a stranger, remove them from the only place and people they had ever known, drop them off with a stranger and then become the main decision-maker in their life until their parents or a parental figure were able to establish permanency for them. I felt like the antagonist of the story.

My friends would often ask me if I was going to have more children. "What do you mean?" I responded. "I have twelve of them." On average, I had anywhere from eight to fifteen children on my caseload, almost all of them being in the custody of our agency. My heart and soul took on the responsibility and commitment of being the parental figure for both them and their parents. It got to the point where my work became my life. I would answer calls from foster parents, kiddos, law enforcement and parents at all hours of the night and 365 days of the year. I had fully dedicated myself and all of my resources to Jaydon and the families I worked with. I was constantly researching new ideas on how to support Jaydon and the families I worked with, and in the end, there was nothing left for myself and my own healing. It was not until later that I found out how much that was needed.

Early on, I was a part of a master's level training on trauma and how our own upbringing impacts how we parent today. One of the articles assigned was called "Ghosts in the Nursery" (Fraiberg et al., 1975). This is when it fully clicked for me that the parents I was working with didn't just need to quit using drugs, quit abusing their children or quit neglecting them. In fact, they were doing the best they could with what they knew; they were essentially parenting in the manner in which they had been parented. Instead, they needed to be seen and heard as the screaming child they themselves had inside. From there, I started to take a deeper interest in working with drug addicted parents and becoming a representation of the stable parent in their life that their own inner child needed.

I attended every training I could find for a deeper understanding of reconnecting with that inner child and becoming the parent that child needed. Over time, I found the restrictions placed on the social work practice in the county and public sectors very limiting from having the true human connection that could create impact.

I challenged the status quo. I knew that to truly heal the inner child, I could not disappear, so I did not. When cases closed, I always continued to be there for my clients whenever they called. Yet again, work continued to consume my life. I was not doing my own internal work. Instead, I was constantly pouring into others. That can only last for so long before something destructs. And then it did: *I fell apart.*

I was thirty-two and faced with my own reality; my entire life was being flipped upside-down and I was getting a divorce. I lost everything. I realized I had built a life filled with external happiness by filling everyone else's cup. I placed my worth on what I did for others or the way I looked to others. I completely self-destructed. I was miserable and lost. I had lost connection with my inner child.

Even at work, people I worked with viewed and treated me differently because they could see the self-destruction and unhealthy behaviors. I no longer knew who I was. I then realized I never knew who I was. After attempting to take my own life, I never healed myself internally. I felt like I was in a void. And because I lacked a sense of self-worth and harbored fears of judgment, I met my needs through external things such as status, houses, cars, and other material things.

I took great pride in ensuring those around me were thriving, but truly inside I was only surviving. The divorce brought on the full spotlight, and I was unable to run from it anymore. At first, instead of addressing it and doing the work, I decided subconsciously that I was going to prove that I was unworthy of anything. I engaged in behaviors that were dangerous and completely out of character for me.

It was interesting to be working in a field of human connection as I self-destructed. We are taught to believe in others' ability to change and to hold out hope for them when they cannot do it themselves. Yet here I was self-destructing, and instead of being viewed as worthy of change, I felt as though I was constantly being watched and judged by those around me because in all reality I was doing it to myself. It was hard to hold hope for myself, but I was able to hold out hope for my clients. This was the one time I could feel worthy again. I was in the human connection with my clients because I not only could hear them and see them, but I could also understand their pain on a level I never had before.

My clients had no clue that my life was self-destructing because my non-destructive time and the times I felt most like myself was when I was in connection with them and holding out hope.

Meanwhile, working in a government job comes with a shit ton of paperwork and I fell drastically behind. My ability to focus on much of anything aside from human connection was nonexistent. I was finally called out by my supervisors and was actually told I was no longer respected as a social worker. That statement was the icing on the cake. It hurt me to the core, but it also reiterated to my subconscious that my current behaviors were working: they were proving that I was unworthy.

I felt reaffirmed but also trapped. I was in a profession where we are taught to focus on people's strengths and to believe that they truly want to do good. Now, in this industry, I was a worker not worthy of receiving that same understanding. Instead of being the social worker, I needed a social worker.

But that was not the worst part. I also was failing at my commitment to my son who at the time was fifteen years old just entering high school. I was no longer a role model for him. I was no longer able to protect him from pain and suffering. My actions and reaction to the divorce caused an even deeper pain in him. I was absent from his life and allowed him to fall apart without access to my love, because at that time my love was completely unavailable to myself and anyone around me. When I would attempt to spend time with him, it was a reminder of my greatest failure and I would take it out on him. I would say things that hurt us both deeply and was unable to connect with him through love and understanding. I was empty, angry, and filled with shame and guilt. He began to push away as well and went down his own path of destruction.

Again, suicide became a regular part of my daily thoughts—but this time it was different. Instead of doing something that would instantly end my journey here, I subconsciously surrounded myself with people, places and things that would create the environment for a slow, painful death. I had failed again. I was saved once for what I thought was the reason to dedicate my life to others, and I had failed. I was unable to even hold up that end of the deal, so I deserved to suffer a death physically, emotionally and mentally.

I had always prided myself in being a leader that my coworkers would go to. But that was no longer the case. Instead, I was the one that was talked about when I left the room. I was the one that others were concerned about. It was no longer a supportive environment. Instead of reaching out a caring hand, they would go straight to their superiors. I was placed on a performance improvement plan and required to do reflective supervision. This was no longer Ashley Abramson. I was a stranger in my own body.

I again saw this as an opportunity for them to gather additional information to get me out of there, so I employed one of my strongest coping skills and did anything and everything to avoid it. The supervisor came to realize I was purposely avoiding the reflective supervision with her, and she immediately scheduled the date and time we would be meeting. I was very apprehensive to meet with her. Surprisingly, when I entered the room, I had an overwhelming feeling of safety. I was being truly seen as a soul and not as the train wreck I had become; she was able to see me in my purest form.

She was for me what I had been for so many over the years. She became the safe, stable adult in my life that provided me with unconditional love. I needed that to heal my own inner child. She was the first person who truly allowed me to be me and share the darkest sides of me without judgment—only love, compassion and hope were welcomed. She was my light, my hope. And she carried me when I could not do it on my own.

I had spent so many years providing the support and safe space for others to not only survive but thrive, and had forgotten about my own inner child who was barely surviving. She was lost, broken, and almost to the point of unresponsiveness. I had provided a safe space for healing in others for so long that I had forgotten that as a helper, I needed help just as much.

I would ask myself, "How could I be worthy of helping others when I didn't even know how to help myself?" My supervisor showed me the way. She provided me a safe space to fully explore that inner child. When I messed things up, she still always showed me I was worthy of love. Over time, I became stronger and began to walk beside her, and eventually she walked behind me on this journey.

As I began to heal more and more, I began to become a version of myself I never knew was possible. I was filled with light, hope, love, and pure joy. Though I was again filled with this light, I was now in a system that was not in alignment with it. I was not able to give myself the same grace as I was expected to give my clients, the grace of people being capable of change and worthy of the opportunity to be seen. That is when I set out on a mission to leave my profession as a social worker and create a platform that has the full space to create the deep supportive human connection truly needed for long-term transformation.

I developed a path for others back home to their inner child through what I call "The Unicorn Effect". I utilize my skills and knowledge of the inner child and trauma from over a decade in the field of child protection. I fully poured my heart and soul into creating a safe container for women to reconnect with their inner child and rewrite the narratives that they were living by. Within two months, I was ready to leave the system that taught me so much, contributed to my destruction, and provided the human connection. I needed to heal my own inner child.

Today, I am fully living in my purpose, my light is shining as bright as the day it came into this world, I dance in the streets when everyone is watching, and I don't give an F. I honor that not everyone is meant to be in my life instead of changing myself to fit their mold. Be prepared for me to ask you a million questions when I meet you because I am genuinely curious about you and your views. I am constantly testing the boundaries that I am faced with; not to be a "rebel", but instead to allow myself and others to see that there is always another way if we just open our hearts and minds to it. I can envision this world in such a brighter place than it is today, and I am going to do everything in my power to provide that safe place for others to heal, question, and test the boundaries they are currently living by.

I want you to know that as hard as life gets in the darkest of days when you feel alone and vulnerable, that inner child is in there waiting for you to unlock the door. By reconnecting with our inner child, we have the ability to not only rewrite history but have an impact on the generations to come. I always knew I was meant to work with the children of the world. I never imagined that my own inner child would be the one who needed me the most.

Pearl of Wisdom
"You are meant to be seen as your most magical self."
~ Ashley Abramson

ABOUT THE AUTHOR

Ashley is a Mentor for Divorced Women. She mentors the raw woman after divorce to discover newfound confidence and joy by rebuilding her purpose-filled life from the ground up.

After a 15 year relationship Ashley found her life flipped upside down through divorce. She was hopeless, broken, lost and alone. The focus of her profession at the time was healing the inner children of her clients. That's when she realized she needed to heal her own inner child.

Her goal is to blend her wisdom and expertise of the impact childhood traumas have on adults and her own experience to rebuild and heal after divorce. She uses a strengths-based approach to help women find their magically authentic selves after divorce.

Ashley believes that you are Divorced not Destroyed and that every woman deserves to live her most magical life . Her podcast, The Unicorn Effect, provides the support for whatever shit is pulling you down that day. Ashley is also an international best-selling author.

Website: https://linktr.ee/TheUnicornEffect

ABOUT EXALTED PUBLISHING HOUSE

EXALTED Publishing House produces books that move hearts and minds.

We are an *indie book publisher* for leaders, CEOS, entrepreneurs, business owners and organizations who want to get more eyes on their stories.

Founded by Bridget Aileen Sicsko in 2020, Exalted Publishing House has a simple philosophy: change the world through words. Our aim is to work with a small number of entrepreneurs, organizations and businesses each year to uphold the highest standard of intimacy and personalization in the cathartic writing and publishing process. We mainly work in the realms of the alternative, disenfranchised & different by sharing stories that aren't always spoken through mainstream channels.

Corporate Books

We create multi-author books for business owners, CEOS and organizations to highlight the stories of their mission, brand, teams and employees.

Multi-Author Books & Visibility Projects

We work with leaders and entrepreneurs who want to get featured in top tier publications and podcasts and share their story to elevate their brand.

If you would like to purchase a 100+ bulk order of any of our books for schools, organizations, teams, book clubs at a discounted rate, please contact bridget@ bridgetaileen.com for details and prices.

Others Books by Exalted Publishing House

Legacy Speaks, Powerhouse Women Leading Lives Worth Remembering

Success Codes, Secrets To Success You Weren't Taught In School

Lineage Speaks, Women Who Carry The Torch For Future Generations

Coming soon...

Prosperity Codes, How To Attune To and Attract Wealth, Joy and Abundance

Divinity Speaks, Women Who Tune In and Trust Divine Inspiration

REFERENCES

Chapter 3: *Teya F. Dahle*

National Association of Social Workers [NASW]. (2021). *Code of ethics of the National Association of Social Workers*. Retrieved February 27, 2022 from, https://www.socialworkers.org/About/Ethics/Code-of-Ethics/Code-of-Ethics-English

Pawl, J. & St. John, M. (1998). *How you are is as important as what you do in making a positive difference for infants, toddlers and their families*. Washington, D.C.: Zero to Three.

Chapter 6: *Gilbert Domally*

Campbell, C. A., Howard, D., Rayford, B. S., & Gordon, D. M. (2015). Fathers matter: involving and engaging fathers in the child welfare system process. *Children and Youth Services Review, 53*, 84–91. https://doi.org/10.1016/j.childyouth.2015.03.020

Esaki, N., & Larkin, H. (2013). Prevalence of Adverse Childhood Experiences (ACEs) among Child Service Providers. *Families in Society: The Journal of Contemporary Social Services, 94*(1), 31–37. https://doi.org/10.1606/1044-3894.4257

Lackie, B. (1983). The families of origin of social workers. *Clinical Social Work Journal, 11*(4), 309–322. https://doi.org/10.1007/bf00755898

McCubbin, H. I., & Patterson, J. M. (1983). The Family Stress Process. *Marriage & Family Review, 6*(1–2), 7–37. https://doi.org/10.1300/j002v06n01_02

Rosino, M. (2016). ABC-X Model of Family Stress and Coping. *Encyclopedia of Family Studies*, 1–6. https://doi.org/10.1002/9781119085621.wbefs313

Chapter 8: *Jess Hoeper*

Morrison, T., (1990), The Emotional Effects of Child Protection on the Worker, Practice 4 (4), p262-4

Chapter 10: *Hilary N. Weaver*

Indigenous peoples. (2005, January 1). INTERNATIONAL FEDERATION OF SOCIAL WORKERS. https://www.ifsw.org/indigenous-peoples/

United Nations. (2007). *United Nations Declaration on the Rights of Indigenous Peoples*. https://www.un.org/development/desa/indigenouspeoples/wp-content/uploads/sites/19/2018/11/UNDRIP_E_web.pdf

Weaver, H., Sloan, L., Barkdull, C., & Lee, P. (2021). *CSWE Statement of Accountability and Reconciliation for Harms Done to Indigenous and Tribal Peoples*. Council on Social Work Education. https://cswe.org/getattachment/Education-Resources/Indigenous-and-Tribal-Content/CSWE-Statement-of-Accountability-and-Reconciliation-for-Harms-Done-to-Indigenous-and-Tribal-Peoples.pdf.aspx

Wikipedia contributors. (2021, December 3). Jewel Freeman Graham. Wikipedia. https://en.wikipedia.org/wiki/Jewel_Freeman_Graham

YS News Staff. (2019, March 8). *Al Denman*. The Yellow Springs News. https://ysnews.com/news/2019/01/al-denman

Chapter 12: *Daniel Martin*

Blackstock, Cindy et al. (2011). *First Peoples Child and Family Review*, vol. 6, no. 1. First Nations Child and Family Caring (35-46)

Merriam-Webster. (n.d.). Conscience. In *Merriam-Webster.com dictionary*. Retrieved March 4, 2022, from https://www.merriam-webster.com/dictionary/conscience

Rethinking foster care: Molly McGrath Tierney at TEDxBaltimore 2014. (2014, February 27). [Video]. YouTube. https://www.youtube.com/watch?v=c15hy8dXSps

White, E. B. (1952). *Charlotte's Web* (1st ed.). HarperCollins.

Chapter 18: *Michael McKnight*

Anglin, J. P. (2003). *Pain, Normality, and the Struggle for Congruence: Reinterpreting Residential Care for Children and Youth (CHILD & YOUTH SERVICES)* (1st ed.). Routledge.

Brendtro, L. K., & Mitchell, M. L. (2022). *Deep Brain Learning: evidence-based essentials in education, treatment, and youth development.* Starr Commonwealth.

Dana, D., & Porges, S. W. (2018). *The Polyvagal Theory in Therapy: Engaging the Rhythm of Regulation (Norton Series on Interpersonal Neurobiology)* (Illustrated ed.). W. W. Norton & Company.

Ellis, W., & Dietz, W. (2017). A New Framework for Addressing Adverse Childhood and Community Experiences: The Building Community Resilience Model.. *Academic Pediatrics, 17* (7S). http://dx.doi.org/10.1016/j.acap.2016.12.011

Felitti V. J. (2002). The Relation Between Adverse Childhood Experiences and Adult Health: Turning Gold into Lead. *The Permanente journal, 6*(1), 44–47.

Hobbs, N. (1982). *The Troubled and Troubling Child (Jossey-Bass Social and Behavioral Science Series)* (First Edition). Jossey-Bass Publishers.

Hooks, B. (1994). *Teaching to Transgress: Education as the Practice of Freedom (Harvest in Translation)*. Routledge.

Kanov, J. M., Maitlis, S., Worline, M. C., Dutton, J. E., Frost, P. J., & Lilius, J. M. (2004). Compassion in Organizational Life. *American Behavioral Scientist, 47*(6), 808–827. https://doi.org/10.1177/0002764203260211

Long, N. J., Fecser, F. A., Morse, W. C., Newman, R. G., & Long, J. E. (2014). *Conflict in the Classroom: Successful Behavior Management Using the Psychoeducational Model* (7th ed.). Pro Ed.

Long, N. J., Wood, M. M., & Fecser, F. A. (2001). *Life Space Crisis Intervention: Talking With Students in Conflict, 2nd Edition* (2nd ed.). Pro-Ed.

Mate, D. G. (2019, June 14). *Dr Gabor Maté on Childhood Trauma, The Real Cause of Anxiety, Our "Insane" Culture and Ayahuasca* [Video]. YouTube. https://www.youtube.com/watch?v=e7pV0IPWUlI

Perry, B. D., & Szalavitz, M. (2017). *The Boy Who Was Raised as a Dog: And Other Stories from a Child Psychiatrist's Notebook -- What Traumatized Children Can Teach Us About Loss, Love, and Healing* (1st ed.). Basic Books.

Rogers, C. (1980). *A Way of Being* (1st ed.). Houghton Mifflin.

Tobin, L. (1991). *What Do You Do with a Child Like This?: Inside the Lives of Troubled Children*. Whole Person Associates.

van der Kolk, V., MD. (2015). *The Body Keeps the Score: Brain, Mind, and Body in the Healing of Trauma* (Reprint ed.). Penguin Publishing Group.

Chapter 24: *Ashley Abramson*

Fraiberg, S., Adelson, E., & Shapiro, V. (1975). Ghosts in the Nursery. *Journal of the American Academy of Child Psychiatry*, *14*(3), 387–421. https://doi.org/10.1016/s0002-7138(09)61442-4

FURTHER ASSISTANCE

If you or someone you know is struggling or needs help, please know you are not alone and seek the help you need.

Suicide Prevention Hotline:

United States: 1-800-273-8255

Better Help: https://www.betterhelp.com/

CPSIA information can be obtained
at www.ICGtesting.com
Printed in the USA
BVHW031708061222
653569BV00014B/1191